Developing Children's Emotional Intelligence

Also available from Continuum

100 Ideas for Supporting Pupils with Social, Emotional and Behavioural Difficulties – Roy Howarth
Behavioural, Emotional and Social Difficulties – Janet Kay
Handbook of Social, Emotional and Behavioural Difficulties – Morag Hunter-Carsch, Rosemary Sage, Yonca Tiknaz and Paul Cooper

Available from Network Continuum

7 Successful Strategies to Promote Emotional Intelligence in the Classroom – Marziyah Panju
Emotional Intelligence and Enterprise Handbook – Cheryl Buggy
Pocket PAL: Emotional Intelligence – Steve Bowkett

Developing Children's Emotional Intelligence

Shahnaz Bahman and Helen Maffini

continuum

Continuum International Publishing Group

The Tower Building	80 Maiden Lane, Suite 704
11 York Road	New York,
London SE1 7NX	NY 10038

www.continuumbooks.com

British Library Cataloguing-in-Publication Data
A catalogue record for this book is available from the British Library.

ISBN: 978 0 82649 9 745 (paperback)

Library of Congress Cataloging-in-Publication Data
Bahman, Shahnaz.
    Developing children's emotional intelligence / Shahnaz Bahman and Helen Maffini.
        p. cm.
    Includes bibliographical references.
    ISBN 978-0-8264-9974-5
    1. Learning, Psychology of. 2. Classroom environment. 3. Emotional intelligence–Activity programs. I. Maffini, Helen. II. Title.
        LB1060.B34 2008
        370.15'34–dc22
                                                            2008019065

Typeset by YHT Ltd, London
Printed and bound in Great Britain by Cromwell Press, Wiltshire

Acknowledgement

Many thanks to:

Our editor, Alison Clark for all her encouragement and support throughout the process of writing this book

Gareth Dewar for his help in proof reading the book

Josh Freedman for his endorsement of this book

Alison Lever for her support during the writing process

Heidi Arnold, Charmaine D'Costa, Yousra Ahmed, Stephanie, Maha Younes and Nadia Mohamed for their feedback and reflections

The many children who inspired us and helped us to improve the activities in this book

Dedication

I dedicate this book to my mother Frances, whom I miss dearly. She taught me to have empathy and to be compassionate, a gift I hope to pass on to my own daughters, Alexandra and Francesca. I would like to thank my husband Giampaolo for all his love and support

Helen Maffini

To my daughter Eman and my son Hussein for being who they are, making me proud every day, and to my husband Adel for always being there to support me along life's beautiful road

Shahnaz Bahman

Contents

Preface

We wrote this book with the hope that we could share some of our experiences of teaching emotional intelligence to children in a practical and stimulating manner that can easily be integrated into most classrooms.

We are both passionate about the subject and believe the first step in educating any child must be to create a feeling of safety, security and wellbeing. Only then will true learning take place.

We met each other by chance three years ago when Helen moved to Bahrain. Immediately finding common ground on many educational issues, we began working on several projects, including this book! We were fortunate to be able to travel to several international conferences together to present some of the ideas in this book.

A deep friendship resulted, and although we now live in different countries, we are still collaborating via the internet, phone calls and the occasional visit.

In this book, we will look at the different tools that you as teachers or educators can use to help children enhance their emotional intelligence. The tools are practical and have all been tried and tested. We have added a teacher's reflection whenever possible to throw more light on their application and outcomes.

The first chapter examines the term Emotional Intelligence (EQ) and its background. An introduction follows of how to develop your EQ skills as a teacher. An emotionally intelligent teacher is a great asset to the whole teaching and learning experience. Such teachers can have a great and positive impact upon the lives of the children they teach. The next section is about creating a positive learning environment, without which all attempts will fail as, if children do not feel safe, secure and interested in what we do, there will be a negative impact upon learning. The rest of the book is dedicated to the tools and strategies that teachers can use to enhance children's EQ. After reading the first three chapters, you may choose to dip in and out of chapters to gather ideas, there is no need to read the book sequentially beyond those chapters. Clear guidelines and stimulating hands-on activities enrich the book and help to make the learning experience a worthwhile one. An EQ theory link section follows, where we relate the activities to Goleman's (1995) framework of EQ components.

Throughout the book we have used the term him, his or he to simplify, but we mean both male and female children. All the activities we suggest are suitable for boys or girls. We have also chosen to use the term EQ for emotional intelligence, although the use of EI is also interchangeable with the term emotional intelligence.

We hope that the ideas introduced in this book will help to make a difference in children's lives and further help children achieve success both in school and in their lives outside the classroom. Our contribution to the children's world might be small, but we are doing it with great love. As Mother Teresa said, 'We cannot do great things in this life, but we can do small things with great love.'

We would love to hear of any ideas you would like to share.

Please contact us:

Helen Maffini: ghmaffini@hotmail.com or ghmaffini@gmail.com

Shahnaz Bahman: shahnazbahman@hotmail.com

1

The Big Picture

Teaching and learning are about problem solving. Education is the process by which you put teachers and learners in the best possible environment for them to do this together.

Dennis Littky

The only really substantial thing education can do is help us to become continuous, life-long learners.

Dennis Littky

All learning has an emotional base.

Plato

The challenges children face

It is difficult not to feel concerned about what children go through in these busy times on so many different levels. Some face great challenges from issues that not only hinder their academic achievement but also, in extreme cases, can challenge their basic survival.

A glance at the world news reveals a long list of difficult situations: child abuse, high divorce rates, child pregnancy, drug addictions, illnesses related to body image, violence, suicide and bullying, to name a few. Society needs to consider what responsibility educators have in making a difference in the lives of children. Can we equip children with the knowledge and skills that they need to be successful in life? Or, on the other hand, is school only about the teaching of academic subjects? What goals should a school be working towards?

What should schools focus on?

Reflecting on school performance and taking into account the huge pressures that they face in all aspects of their operations, the main focus for many schools has become academic progress, the curriculum, meeting standards in different subjects, finishing the textbook, gathering evidence of achievement, carrying out tests and exams, calculating grades and writing reports. Many schools hold teachers accountable only for the academic achievement of their students, and place little or no emphasis on the social and emotional growth of these children.

What about the whole child? What about the development of the skills that these children need in order to manage themselves effectively and to go forward in life? What about the development of their emotional and social skills? McCown, Freedman, Jensen and Rideout (1998: ix) suggest that 'Education has given little systematic attention to the positive emotional development of children'. We believe that all children deserve to be taught emotional intelligence skills in their daily school life.

Why EQ?

Developing children's emotional intelligence can play a great role not only in their character growth, but in their academic learning as well. There is now a growing body of research that shows that children's academic performance improves when social and emotional factors are dealt with explicitly (Petrides, Frederickson, Furnham, 2004). In fact, current research corroborates that success is as much as 70–80 per cent based on emotional intelligence. In fact, even 'objective' statistics derived from SAT tests and IQ scores draw parallels with emotional intelligence (McCown *et al.*, 1998). Elias, Arnold and Hussey (2003: 4) find that without EQ development, schools cannot prepare children for academic and real-life success. They go on to say that 'EQ is the missing piece in true reform of education and preparation of students for academic and real life success'.

To provide a sound education for children and equip them with the right skills and tools that enable them to enhance their academic achievements and real-life skills, schools need to go beyond academics and pay serious attention to developing children's emotional intelligence. Elias *et al.* (2003: 4) state that 'Schools that see as their mission the joint and synergistic development of EQ+IQ must become the standard of education.'

What is EQ? How can it be developed in children?

The concept of emotional intelligence is not new. Howard Gardner referred to interpersonal intelligence and intrapersonal intelligence in his theory of multiple intelligences presented in his book *Frames of Mind* (1983). However, Peter Salovey of Yale University and Jack Mayer of the University of New Hampshire were the first to use the term Emotional Intelligence, while they were researching the factors behind effective functioning in society (Mayer and Salovey, 1997). It was Daniel Goleman in his book *Emotional Intelligence* (1995), who brought the concept to the general public.

Various authors define emotional intelligence differently, and research continues to refine the concept of EQ. Some of the existing definitions are very scientific. We find that the most practical definition comes from Six Seconds, a global EQ organization, that says 'Emotional intelligence is consciously choosing thoughts, feelings and actions to get optimal results in your relationships with yourself and others' (Freedman and Jensen, 2005).

Goleman (1995) explains the five domains of emotional intelligence:

1. Knowing one's emotions: Self-awareness is the keystone of emotional intelligence. It is the ability to recognize feelings as they happen in real-life situations.

2. Managing emotions: Handling feelings appropriately is an ability that builds on self-awareness. It is being able to manage strong feelings so that we can soothe ourselves, maintain balance and not be overwhelmed or paralyzed by them.

3. Motivating oneself: Self-motivation and mastery is about being goal-oriented, keeping focused and channelling emotions toward desired results. It leads to being highly effective and productive.

4. Recognizing emotions in others: Empathy is the fundamental people skill. It means being able to recognize emotions in others and understand others' point of view.

5. Handling relationships: Managing emotions in others is the art of relationships. It is the ability to handle a range of social relationships and to interact smoothly with others.

Emotional development in early childhood

Researchers have advanced the work on emotional development over the last two decades. Henniger (1999) wrote 'Emotional development in young children consists of a gradual growth in the ability to recognize, label and appropriately respond to their feelings. Each of these steps is important to their emotional health and must be learned through repeated interactions with others' (p. 340). Nabuzoka and Smith (1995) found that the capacity to recognize and comprehend emotions develops, as we grow older. They indicate children as young as three can identify sadness, happiness and fear via non-verbal indications, body language, gestures such as facial expression and tone of voice.

The National Research Council and Institute of Medicine (2000) illustrates that the essential developments of healthy, stimulating interactions in early childhood should include the concepts of contingency and reciprocity. Contingency and reciprocity describes when the relationship between young children and their caregivers are harmonious with each other so caregivers can deduce children's emotional signals and react in an appropriate way to meet the child's needs.

Caregivers in preschools and daycares can stimulate emotional growth through everyday classroom activities. By carefully planning a curriculum that encourages children to explore their feelings through imaginative media and make-believe play, healthy emotional growth can occur.

Emotional development in elementary school

Two decades of research has shown us that children's emotional and social skills connect to their academic achievements. For many children, academic achievement in the elementary years appears to build on a firm foundation of children's emotional and social skills (Ladd, Kochenderfer and Coleman, 1997). Teachers who are aware of these links can do more to enable them. Jensen (2005) informs us that emotional development continues as children develop more of an interest in social sensibilities and friendships. As teachers, we need to capture these opportunities to develop children's emotional intelligence.

Teachers need to realize the power of emotions and how this can affect children's retention of information. Worksheets and textbooks full of facts are not going to stimulate many emotions from this age group. Elementary school children are curious and ready to explore the real world. Hands-on activities, re-enactments, discussions and artistic expression tend to enhance the emotional connections to the curriculum and are excellent tools for children in the six to ten age ranges.

The Collaborative for Academic, Social, Emotional Learning (CASEL, 2007) indicate that in relation to Goleman's (1995) framework children of Elementary school age should be able to do the following in relation to each aspect:

- Self-awareness: children of this age group should be able to identify and accurately name basic emotions such as happiness, sadness and anger.

- Self-management: we expect children to be able to explain the procedure of establishing and working towards their own goals.

- Social awareness: we expect children to be able to recognize verbal, physical and situational signals suggesting how others feel.

- Relationship skills: children should be able to explain methods to building and maintaining friendships.

What can teachers do to support this emotional development?

We have adapted this list of suggestions from Dettore and Cleary (1997/98).

1. Recognize children's emotional responses as valid
2. Model suitable expressions of emotion
3. Display empathy
4. Provide children the required time, space and materials to explore emotional challenges
5. Assist children to expand their verbal skills in order to cope with difficult circumstances
6. Support children as they build connections with their prior experiences in order to manage new challenges

Recommended reading

Elias, M. J., Arnold, H. and Hussey, C. S. (2003) *EQ+IQ; Best Leadership Practices for Caring and Successful Schools*. Thousand Oaks, CA: Corwin Press.

Ellison, L. (2001) *The Personal Intelligences*. Thousand Oaks, CA: Corwin Press.

Gardner, H. (1983) *Frames of Mind; The Theory of Multiple Intelligences*. New York: Basic Books.

Goleman, D. (1995) *Emotional Intelligence*. New York: Bantam.

McCown, K. S., Freedman, J. M., Jensen, A. L. and Rideout, M. C. (1998) *Self Science; The Emotional Intelligence Curriculum*. San Mateo, CA: Six Seconds.

2 Becoming an Emotionally Intelligent Teacher

> When dealing with people, remember you are not dealing with creatures of logic, but creatures of emotion.
>
> Dale Carnegie

> What the teacher is, is more important than what he teaches.
>
> Karl Menninger

A tale of two classrooms

Ms Walker and Ms Parker's classrooms were across the hall from each other, yet they couldn't have been further apart in terms of being emotionally intelligent classrooms.

Ms Walker always had a smile for her students and a welcoming gesture. If a child looked a bit down, she would take them aside and talk with them with respect and kindness. She was aware of her tone of voice, her eye movement and posture, and their effects on her students. Ms Walker was a teacher who cared about her students both in and out of the classroom. Ms Parker, on the other hand, believed that her job was to cover the curriculum. She could not tolerate noise in the classroom or children acting silly and misbehaving. Ms Parker was a teacher whose students felt afraid of her. At times, they even felt scared to speak up in her classroom.

A child, Lizzie, in Ms Walker's class was going through the divorce of her parents. Lizzie started to withdraw and act quietly. Ms Walker quietly spoke to Lizzie in a manner that allowed her to open up. She took books out of the library for Lizzie about divorce and encouraged her to write about her feelings in a journal. Ms Walker kept in touch with both Lizzie's parents to make sure they understood the impact on

Lizzie. Lizzie knew in her heart that Ms Walker was always there if she needed to talk to someone.

Across the hall in Ms Parker's class, Ben's mother had just had twins. Ms Parker however, was only mildly aware of the fact, not wishing to 'get involved' in matters that had nothing to do with her. This morning she had shouted at Ben, telling him that lately he had not been doing his homework properly. She hadn't realized the emotions he was experiencing and the lack of time his mother had for him with two newborns in the house. Ben felt embarrassed and angry when she shouted at him and withdrew from participating in the class that day. The more Ms Parker belittled him, the worse he felt. He stopped doing his homework altogether as he knew Ms Parker would not be happy with his work even if he tried.

Ms Walker had read up on emotional intelligence and how important it was for children to feel safe, secure and nurtured before true learning could take place. In Ms Parker's class on the other hand children sometime were 'emotionally hijacked' when she shouted furiously at them, or glared at a child for forgetting his homework. You as teachers have a profound effect on children's life. We might not always remember what we learnt in school, but we can't forget those affectionate teachers who touched our hearts and soul. If it weren't for those teachers, perhaps we wouldn't have written this book. 'One looks back with appreciation to brilliant teachers, but with gratitude to those who touched our human feelings.' (Jung as cited in Ellison, 2001)

In this chapter, we shall discuss the characteristics of an emotionally intelligent teacher, adapting the framework Goleman introduced in 1995. We shall look into the five domains of self-awareness, managing emotions, motivating oneself, recognizing emotion in others and handling relationships.

Self-awareness

Self-awareness is the cornerstone in developing any teacher's emotional intelligence. 'This awareness of emotions is the fundamental emotional competence on which others such as emotional self-control is built' (Goleman, 1995: 51). Self-awareness is knowing what is happening and how we think and feel about it, rather than being immersed in a situation and not knowing we are in it at the time. As Goleman (1995:51) states, 'Self awareness in short means being aware of both our mood and our thoughts about the mood'.

Developing self-awareness is a vital skill for teachers. When you have good self-knowledge, you can better understand your students, and when you understand your students, you can definitely teach them better.

> Knowing my students and my subject depends heavily on self-knowledge. When I don't know myself, I cannot know who my students are. I will see them through a glass darkly. In the shadows of my unexamined life – and when I cannot see them clearly, I cannot teach them well. (Palmer, 1998:2)

However, the danger lies in the fact that whether we have good or poor self-awareness, we reflect that back on our students. We are always under our students' magnifying glasses, where they look at us closely while we are carried away with all the tasks at hand. We exude our emotions and thoughts to our students' whether we are aware of it or not. 'We are teaching one thing or another all of the time, because we are constantly radiating what we are' (Covey, 1992: 126).

The children in our classes don't always learn what we want them to learn from us. We often hear teachers complaining that children don't listen to what they say. In fact, children learn from what we do much more than what we say as Childre (1996: 11) wrote so eloquently 'what we are teaches the child far more than what we say, so we must be what we want our children to become'.

Consequently, if we want to teach children to be emotionally intelligent, we first need to *be* emotionally intelligent. If we want them to have good self-awareness, we need to have good self-awareness. Ellison (2001: 16) sums it up with this statement 'I cannot give what I don't have. My success with students depends on my own personal intelligence.'

Developing self-awareness

Self-awareness involves a set of sub-skills. That is, recognition of feelings, understanding how these feelings impact on us, and being able to use that knowledge to manage the feelings effectively, for example by choosing to act more positively (Sharp, 2001).

When we don't have self-awareness we can easily fall into the trap of being what Goleman (1995) calls 'emotionally hijacked'. That is when we are not aware of how we feel and we are caught up in strong reactive acts. It is evident that the less self-aware we are, the more likely we are to be emotionally hijacked. We have all seen examples of situations when fellow teachers lose control over their feelings. In some cases, this loss of control ends up severely affecting children's well-being.

One way of developing your self-awareness is through observing yourself in different situations. Keeping a journal can be a good idea, where you can reflect on your feelings and see how self-aware you are. Journaling is a tool that takes time to see benefits. Reflection and other skills that come from journaling are beneficial to teachers as they start to realize what triggers their emotions and how to ensure they best manage the situations when they feel emotionally stressed.

Another idea is to observe our physical status. Our bodies communicate to us all the time. Scanning our bodies mentally to see how we feel in different situations can be very informative. For example, how do you feel when something disturbing happens in class? What happens to your facial expression, your heartbeat, does your skin colour flush and do you start fidgeting? Your body gives you precious information that you shouldn't neglect. By watching yourself in different situations over a period of time you develop the habit of being self-aware.

Here are some questions that you can ask yourselves to boost your self-awareness:

How do I generally feel about my profession?

How do I feel about school?

What about the subject(s) I teach?

How about my students?

What makes me feel good at school?

What pushes me to the edge?

Do I really have good level of self-awareness?

In situations that disturb me do I have good self-control or am I easily emotionally hijacked?

By getting into the habit of asking ourselves questions that enhance our self-awareness, observing our feelings and reactions to different situations, we can help improve our self-awareness. Once this cornerstone is in place then many other skills will fall into place more smoothly.

Managing emotions

Managing emotions has to do with our ability to handle our feelings appropriately. As we mentioned above, a teacher's lack of self-awareness can result in mismanaging emotions, which leads to unsatisfactory results. It is likely that at times we all have been in situations where we get overwhelmed with negative emotions in our everyday school life. These emotions can range from frustration, anger, stress, fear, anxiety, or even feeling so miserable that we push ourselves to get up in the morning and come to school. Going through negative emotions is a normal process and as Goleman (1995: 63) puts it, 'Downs as well as ups spice life', but adds 'but need to be in balance.' Balance is the key word here. What can we as teachers do to stay balanced or perhaps to feel excited, happy and full of joy and energy most of the time? When we consider that we spend one third of our lives at school and that we are in a profession that makes or breaks the lives of the children, should we not strive for the highest target possible!

To start with, thoughts and feelings are very much interrelated. In other words, the way we perceive things affects how we feel about them. Consequently, if we change our perception our feelings will change accordingly. Change in our thoughts and feelings will lead to changes in our attitude and behaviour. Robin Sharma in *The Monk Who Sold his Ferrari* said 'If you want to live a more peaceful, meaningful life, you must think more peaceful meaningful thoughts.'

When we are in school, we might sometimes feel like we are in a never-ending cycle, as teaching is a very busy, multitasking job. Our profession involves the consumption of a lot of mental and emotional energy. In other words, we are on the move all the time. We do not have much time, if any, to pause and relax or enjoy a bit of total silence. Our brain works through all kinds of issues from covering the curriculum to dealing with social problems to making sure an extracurricular activity is prepared. Therefore, we need to de-junk our brains and to feel balanced again. We can accomplish this through meditation, yoga, prayer or deep breathing. It is highly beneficial to take a few minutes off and be in total silence, sitting quietly in a clean beautiful place, even if this place is in your mind! If your school has a garden, you can take a few minutes off just by having a calm, relaxing short walk, or eating your lunch in relaxing surroundings. These few minutes of a break away from the hectic life of the school can pay off greatly and can help you feel energized, refreshed and ready to meet your students with a welcoming heart and a nice smile rather than a frowning face. This is highly recommended, especially when you are in situations that cause you to have negative emotions such as stress, fatigue, disappointment or frustration.

In schools, things do not always go as planned or expected. As teachers, we experience many situations that might trigger our anger. The danger with anger lies in not having enough self-awareness, so one might climb the escalator of anger without being aware of one's emotions. The level of anger keeps rising until it reaches a peak where we get emotionally hijacked and act in a way that we might regret later. One effective way of managing anger is to choose to pause and to walk away from the situation, cool down in any way you can, such as drinking some water, going for a short walk, changing the topic, or distracting yourself in any way found to be appropriate in that specific situation. When things have cooled down, then you can think of different options that can solve the problem and choose the most appropriate one.

The words we use in our daily life have great influence on how we feel. There is a direct relationship between the language we use and the programming of our brain. Neuro Linguistic Programming (NLP) has become a popular science and it has a lot to offer us. Learning NLP makes one more conscious about the way we think and the language we use. Selecting more positive than negative words can have great impact on our emotions. A good way to see the number of positive or negative words you use is to record yourself in class. Make a list of all the negative words, and see if you can replace them with ones that are more positive. Such practices can have incredible effects on not only your feelings as a teacher but also on the children as every word you say can negatively or positively affect all the children present in the class. Words are very powerful and play great role in making us who we are. Mahatma Ghandi put it beautifully when he said, 'Keep my words positive, words become my behaviour, keep my behaviour positive, behaviour becomes my habits, keep my habits positive, habits become my values, keep my values positive, values become my destiny'.

Self-motivation

We all have dreams. We all have goals to achieve, but the way we march towards these goals might vary greatly among individuals. What comes into play here are our emotions as well as our intellect. Self-motivated people march faster and more enthusiastically towards their goals than the ones who lack self-motivation. On their journey towards reaching their destination self-motivated individuals like everybody else come across some bumps, but they do not get defeated by obstacles. Stress or frustration doesn't overwhelm them. They see problems as learning opportunities; they solve their problems and continue their journey of achieving their targets. When things go off track, they don't blame themselves. They don't label themselves as failures, instead they see the cause to be an area or a strategy that didn't work and they think of doing things differently, following other strategies to make things work. They live with positive attitudes and feel hopeful. While working they manage to reach a level of what Goleman (1995) calls 'flow', which is a state of 'self-forgetness' as a result of being engrossed in the task at hand. At this stage, they achieve excellence effortlessly. For self-motivators, achieving targets is an indispensable joy. They are determined to reach their destination, but if their goals seem to be unrealistic they are flexible enough to change or modify them, drawing up new plans to reach them. For this group of teachers, teaching becomes a passion not just a profession.

Such teachers are indispensable assets to their schools. They have an intense effect not only on their students, but also on other staff members. They radiate their qualities to the people around them. Attitude and mood can be contagious and can have a strong effect on our performance and our teaching in class.

Helping teachers to be self-motivated

We hope that most teachers have chosen teaching because they have a passion for it, and not just because it is a respectable job. It makes a big difference when we enjoy what we are doing rather than having forcibly to drag ourselves to do the job. In both cases, the class is running, but the sense and level of achievement and the impact on the children can be very different. After all, enjoying what you do is something that we owe to ourselves and good education is something we owe to the children we teach.

What shapes our performance has a lot to do with our perception of teaching. We must look at teaching as a precious profession that can help or hinder children's lives in more ways than we can imagine. If we see ourselves as important individuals who are lucky to be in a position to make a difference in the lives of the children in our care, if we can find meaning and value in what we do and if we believe in these values then we can develop the kind of self-motivation that is needed to make a difference. The very fact that you are reading this book expresses your desire to be a teacher who will make a difference.

Our emotions and love for the children will be the strongest asset that we can use to help the children grow and flourish. As Ellison (2001: 5) states, 'I teach children. The children are my focus. This is a very different attitude from "I teach math". My focus makes a world of difference.'

The field of education is beautiful and it is rapidly growing. In the past 15 years, brain research has revolutionized many concepts in education. Teachers must keep up to date professionally by subscribing to professional organizations, reading journals, books, joining online professional courses, attending workshops and conferences and grasping the many other opportunities that exist. Teacher professional development should be a top priority for school leaders and administrators. We have come across school leaders who changed their school into a professional learning community not only through using outside resources such as the ones mentioned above, but also by providing a lot of in-house learning opportunities which didn't cost the school much, for example peer visits among teachers, assigning the more experienced teachers as mentors to take care of novice teachers, coaching and mentoring, in-house training workshops, group discussions, reflection sessions, book groups, sharing books and journals, etc. Teachers are the most important asset in schools and they deserve access to a variety of professional development opportunities. Unfortunately, not all schools see professional development as a top priority, hence, many teachers must take responsibility for their own professional development. Self-motivated teachers are also proactive. They don't wait to enhance their professional development; they create and seek learning opportunities in different ways. To start with, the internet is a great resource with many free learning opportunities. For many teachers financing their professional development opportunities can be a serious problem. An idea around this is that you can keep a portion of your income in a separate account for your own professional development. This is a good idea and it pays off greatly on different levels. After all, up-to-date motivated teachers are much more in demand than limited, bored, demotivated teachers.

All teachers like to work in a school environment that is orderly and organized, and where teachers feel supported, trusted, respected and appreciated. One of the ways to show appreciation to teachers is to provide them with the kind of help and support they need. As mentioned above, Goleman (1995) suggests that the self-motivated teacher works in a 'flow' mood, by which he means that they achieve excellent results naturally without much struggle. He also explains that for anyone to reach this stage of flow they need to have developed the right skills and knowledge. Flow doesn't happen when the task is too easy. This leads to boredom. It also doesn't happen when the task is too challenging. This leads to stress and anxiety. Flow happens when the task is a bit challenging, but the person has the skills and the time to handle it. Schools can help the teacher to enter the world of flow, where excellent teaching can take place effortlessly, and where teachers get so engrossed in their lessons that neither the teacher nor the children want to leave the room when the bell goes. However, to achieve this fascinating level of performance, schools need to plan learning opportunities for their teachers, then mentor and support them.

Empathy

Teaching is a very caring profession, and teachers can have a great influence on how children learn and feel about school. A teacher can cause a child pain and can create pleasure too. One teacher can help a child love school; another can make a child hate school. It all depends on our relationships with the children. One of the main factors influencing the way we work with children is our ability to understand them, to understand how they feel, the way they think, and what messages they are trying to convey to us through their gestures, their tone of voice, or their facial expressions. Not all teachers can relate to this and read children's emotions, but the ones who can are the lucky ones. They are the empathic teachers.

Being an empathic teacher can have great benefits to both the teacher and the children. For the teacher, it makes a big a difference when he is in tune with children, when there is good relationship between them and when there is respect and positive feelings on both sides. Children usually listen to a teacher they like, and some of them might even strive to please this teacher. In addition to this, learning takes place more smoothly as their brains can take in and process information without being blocked or hijacked by emotional issues. Goleman (1995: 111) suggests 'mastering this empathic ability smooths the way for classroom effectiveness', and obviously this leads to better learning outcomes. This makes the teacher feel good about herself and perhaps creates a better feeling of job satisfaction. After all, we all want to feel the results of all our hard work.

When it comes to children, it is evident that the way they feel about their teacher affects their attitude towards school and towards learning. As we have mentioned in the previous chapter there is a strong relationship between emotions and learning. They will also feel safe and secure when they know that they are with a person who can understand them, cares about them, can accept them for who they are, and is there to help and support them when they call for it.

On the other hand, lacking empathy can be of a great disadvantage. 'The failure to register another's feelings is a major deficit in emotional intelligence and a tragic failing in what it means to be human. For all rapport, the root of caring, stems from emotional attunement, from the capacity for empathy' (Goleman, 1995: 109).

In other words, a teacher who lacks empathy cannot really read the non-verbal cues that the children use to convey their messages. He cannot feel how they feel. He cannot see their point of view and as a result, he cannot understand them, connect with them, or reach them. It is as though they are in a different world altogether. Obviously, this is harmful for the children. They might develop negative emotions towards the teacher and towards the school. These children will feel that there is a huge gap between them and the teacher; they cannot connect with him. They will feel that the teacher doesn't understand them and he is not there for them. They feel insecure, afraid of making mistakes or being judged by the teacher. The negative effects will also reach their academic achievements, since their emotional insecurity can get in the way of their learning process.

Being a more empathic teacher

Like all other EQ skills, empathy develops further if we work on it. To start with, the basis of empathy is self-awareness. The more self-aware we are, the better we can read others' feelings. 'The more open we are to our own emotions, the more skilled we will be in reading feelings' (Goleman, 1995).

There is also a strong relationship between empathy and self-approval. Individuals with high self-approval are more empathic than those with low self-approval. Doty (2001) sees self-approval as 'making an agreement with oneself to accept, love, appreciate and support oneself, imperfections and all, at this very minute', and as 'the willingness to hold onto and to celebrate our ethics, our values, our prejudices, our blemishes, our strengths as well as our weaknesses'.

Our self-approval influences the way we interpret our actions, beliefs and experiences. At this point, our thinking habits of being positive or negative come into play. Looking at things from a more positive perspective can contribute to better self-approval. As teachers, we need to be proud of ourselves for being in such a caring, challenging position. We are the people without whom nations can be in jeopardy. Sometimes our sincerity and dedication takes us to a level where we expect ourselves to be perfect. When we do not get the results we strive to achieve, we feel disheartened and might try to find faults in our performance or blame ourselves for our pitfalls. We need to learn to accept ourselves for all we are, embrace our weaknesses and live peacefully with our imperfections. Once we achieve this on a personal level, we can then accept the children we teach for who they are, appreciate all the differences between us and help them to develop better self-acceptance. This will lead us to having children who can be more empathic.

Handling relationships

This skill incorporates all other skills mentioned earlier in this chapter. It starts with our ability to have a positive relationship with ourselves. Our self-awareness, self-knowledge, self-motivation, self-understanding, self-approval, self-appreciation, self-love and self-management greatly affect our relationship with others. In other words, when we have a positive relationship with ourselves we can have positive relationships with others. For any relationship to be smooth, beautiful and peaceful, it requires individuals to be beautiful and peaceful from within. What we show on the outside is a reflection of what we live in the inside. The emotions we have for ourselves and for others is all felt. We transmit our emotions all the time to those around us. 'We send emotional signals in every encounter and those signals affect those we are with' (Goleman, 1995: 111). In other words, as teachers if we are happy with ourselves, the children can feel it. If we are angry with ourselves, we transmit negative emotions and they feel it too. In addition, if we love and accept the children for who they are, they feel it and if we are angry with them or resent them for any reason, they feel that too. Children and adults alike believe in our feelings more than our words. 'Indeed when a person's words disagree with what is conveyed via his tone of voice, gesture, or other non-verbal channel, the emotional truth is in how he says something rather than *what* he says' (Goleman, 1995: 111). Children believe in the non-verbal cues more than words because we express our emotions non-verbally more than verbally. 'Just as the mode of the rational mind is words, the mode of the emotions is in non-verbal' (1995: 111).

Thus, for us to have a positive relationship with the children our love and acceptance should be genuine, otherwise we can save ourselves the efforts of trying to fake a feeling we do not really have.

It is true that we spend most of our time in school with the children we teach, but they are not the only stakeholders of the school community. By the very nature of the profession, we also communicate with other stakeholders, such as the school principal, colleagues, other staff members and parents. However, sometimes things do not always go the way we wish. Conflicts can arise between the teacher and the administration, other colleagues, a parent or even the children. The degree to which a teacher can manage herself and the situation with whatever party is involved here is a sign of her emotional intelligence. Teachers with high emotional intelligence can show signs of emotional maturity and resolve the conflict calmly. Unfortunately, the ones with low emotional intelligence may react to the situation negatively or aggressively, and this reaction might lead to further problems. The problem can then escalate causing negative emotions along the way and in severe situations, it can get out of hand. Of course, the success or failure of any relationship is not the responsibility of one person. It is the responsibility of all stakeholders involved.

The above example tells us clearly that relationship management is about managing emotions, and we can only acquire the art of managing emotions if we are empathic enough, for if we fail to read all the non-verbal signals that the other person is transmitting to us, we definitely cannot respond appropriately. It's like being on the wrong page. 'Handling emotions in someone else – the fine art of relationships – requires the ripeness of two other emotional skills "self-management and empathy"' (Goleman, 1995: 12).

However, when a relationship takes a negative direction it affects our emotions. Talking about teachers in this chapter one might ask: how would you feel in such situations and what effects can this have overall on the learning process of the children in our care?

As human beings, we have one integrated system. Our emotions, our mind and body are all interrelated. Thus, the way we feel and the way we think affects the decisions we make and the actions we take. Consequently, our emotional wellbeing, our relationship with the children and our performance are affected. We then might leave a mark we do not want to leave on children's feelings and learning. As Jonathan Cohen (1999) states so powerfully in *Educating Mind and Hearts*, as quoted in Ellison's *The Personal Intelligences* (p. 11), 'Virtually all learning happens within the context of relationships So, even if we do not consciously intend to influence our children in this manner, the contacts we have with individual students affect how they feel about themselves and what they are learning.'

In conclusion, the gift of being emotionally intelligent teachers can be an indispensable asset to us all. It will help us to be happier, more enthusiastic teachers and will provide us with the tools we need to use to make a difference in the lives of the children we teach. We end with a quote from Mahatma Ghandi 'You must be the change you wish to see in the world!'

Recommended reading

Cohen, J. (2001) *Caring Classrooms/Intelligent Schools*. New York, NY: Teachers College Press.

Morris, E. and Casey, J. (2006) *Developing Emotional Literate Staff – a Practical Guide*. London: Paul Chapman.

Weare, K. (2004) *Developing the Emotionally Literate School*. London: Sage.

Reflective questions

1. How emotionally intelligent are you?
2. What can you do to become more emotionally intelligent?
3. How do you think the children in your class perceive you?
4. What is something you can start doing immediately to improve your classroom atmosphere and environment?
5. What can you start doing to make the children in your class feel safer and more secure?

3 Creating a Positive Learning Environment

I never teach my pupils; I only attempt to provide the conditions in which they can learn.

Albert Einstein

Let's not forget that little emotions are the greatest captains of our lives and we obey them without realizing it.

Vincent Van Gogh

Where there is great love, there are always miracles.

Willa Cather

I'm sick today

'I'm not going to school today. I feel sick. I have a stomach-ache.' This seemed to be James's favourite phrase each morning. His mother hated when she had to wake him up in the morning. She felt nervous every morning before she entered his room. It was starting to be a real nightmare.

Day after day, James's situation got worse. He would get continuous stomach aches and sometimes he would vomit before going to school. James's mother took him to the doctor but he couldn't find anything physically wrong with him. Still, James complained. The doctor had mentioned that perhaps something was bothering James at home or school causing his stomach pains.

James's mother visited the school. As she walked by James's classroom, she noticed the tables and chairs neatly in rows and filled-in worksheets posted on the bulletin boards. The room did not look warm or inviting like his classroom had the year before.

His mother was naturally very concerned. She went to see the school counsellor. After a few meetings with the counsellor, they discovered that James was feeling very uncomfortable with his class teacher. She was irritable and often shouted at other kids, making James feel scared. She didn't have a warm relationship and was not close to her students. Actually, she didn't really know much about them nor did she have any desire to. Her loud voice and threats to report them to their parents were deeply upsetting for James and some of the other children.

The children felt insecure in her class, some like James would switch off and could not think properly during the lesson. He was still nervous and agitated when he got home and even lost interest in having a bedtime story, something that he had previously enjoyed enormously.

It took a lot of hard work and many discussions with the school counsellor to make the teacher realize how James felt. The teacher argued that James must be overly sensitive and that she had no time to 'play mother' to the children; she had a curriculum to cover!

There are many children in James's situation. Children spend up to one third of their day at school. The school and class environment have a profound effect on children's emotional, social and academic well-being and growth. Most teachers know that when children feel safe, happy and cared for they learn more effectively. On the other hand, when they feel scared, insecure or bored, they can lose their appetite for learning. In extreme cases, school life can become a child's nightmare.

Creating and maintaining a positive environment

Creating and maintaining a positive, safe and healthy learning environment must be a top priority for teachers. If the environment is not a positive one, a great deal of teacher effort is wasted.

In this chapter, we shall discuss how we can create and maintain a classroom environment in which children feel emotionally safe and where they have the opportunity to feel the joy of learning, and will look forward to coming to class in the morning. The mastery of such a challenging set of tasks goes back to the teacher. A teacher's knowledge, skills, attitude, values and love for children have a great effect on her ability to create a positive classroom environment.

The child/teacher relationship

The relationship between the children and the teacher has a direct influence upon emotions and learning. As was discussed in Chapter 2, an emotionally intelligent teacher, who is well aware of how her children feel, and who genuinely cares that they all develop to their full potential, emotionally and socially, as well as intellectually, can have a greater influence on a child's life than a teacher whose main concern is to cover the curriculum. Teaching is a uniquely challenging job and very often teachers make do with limited resources and tools, yet we have all come across great teachers who are passionate about teaching and who make things happen in spite of any obstacles. Rebecca Olness (1997: ix) sums it up with this beautiful quote from Dr Haim Ginott: 'Teachers are expected to reach unattainable goals with inadequate tools. The miracle is that at times they accomplish this impossible task.'

Creating an environment where children thrive!

How can we create a positive, safe and healthy learning environment? Initially, the physical aspect of the classroom can have a profound effect on children's feelings and learning. Creating a creative, colourful and interesting classroom environment, decorated with their pictures, achievements, thoughts and feelings can give children the ownership of their classroom. Personalizing the class environment helps the children to feel loved, welcomed, important and accepted for who they are. Teachers need to maintain a system of rejuvenating the class physical appearance on a regular basis. Children's spirits renew when they see their teacher celebrating their little achievements and success continuously and creatively.

There needs to be a harmony between what the teacher is trying to achieve through the classroom's physical environment and how children feel in class. When children are given the emotional security they need, when they feel appreciated, loved, respected and accepted not for their academic achievements or their behaviour but for who they really are, a relationship of trust and mutual respect will be born. This kind of relationship encourages the children to be themselves, to be curious learners, to ask questions, investigate, open up to learning, enjoy being in class and express their feelings, concerns and points of view with no fear or hesitation.

Actions speak louder than words

In some shape or form, children's brains are active all the time. While we are in class, children assess us continuously. They then come to their own judgements about us and how they feel towards us; this affects the decisions they make in relation to their learning process and outcome. Their criteria are what we do, how we make them feel and not necessarily what we say to them. As we often say, 'actions speak louder than words' and this is especially true of teachers. Children read our emotions through observing our body language before we say anything. A frowning face or a loud voice can put them off. Unappreciative, threatening and unkind words can create a high level of stress. In fact, students can become emotionally hijacked, which can have very negative effects on their well-being and their learning processes, as discussed earlier.

Peer relationships

Another factor that has a strong effect on the classroom environment is children's relationships with their peers. When children are on good terms with their peers, they are emotionally more settled; they can work cooperatively and enjoy their learning experience. On the other hand, when they bully and hurt each other, they feel emotionally insecure and can't concentrate as their brain is preoccupied with their emotional issues, and as a result this affects their learning outcomes.

Making sure that there are good relationships between the children is a responsibility that schools do not always take seriously. This is especially true in schools where the focus is only on achieving academic targets. It is very disheartening to see that in some schools children experience serious emotional issues during school hours, yet they are not always lucky enough to meet a teacher with a warm heart to help them. In some cases, when problems occur between children the school staff play the role of a detective to find the child at fault, and apply the kind of punishment found to be most appropriate. In our opinion, schools need to go a long way beyond that. This is a core responsibility of schools and we do not consider it an option. It is the school and teacher's responsibility to create a classroom environment where children genuinely care for each other. We must not overlook bullying problems. Bullying hurts children deeply. It can lead to school drop-out, anxiety, depression and, in a worst-case scenario, even suicide. Emotionally disturbing issues such as bullying should be totally unacceptable not only in school documents but also in the real-life practices in school. These type of initiatives need to be whole-school approaches to ensure maximum effectiveness.

Developing meaningful classroom rules

Learning cannot take place in a chaotic, disorganized classroom environment where there are no clear routines, rules and consequences. Good organization helps the teacher to manage the classroom, which leads to better learning outcomes. Having clear rules is one of the characteristics of effective classroom management. However, to motivate the children to respect and follow classroom rules, they must be involved in establishing these rules. Classroom rules should not be limited to keeping the class clean and tidy, or lining up when it is time to leave the room. It must also include codes of conduct that protect children emotionally and socially. It is important to word these rules in a positive manner not a negative one, to attract that positivity in the classroom. For example, instead of including 'no bullying' or 'no name calling', items can be included such as 'show mutual respect' or 'show appreciation to others'. One wonderful way to make the rules is to create a class pledge that can be posted in the classroom and read aloud each morning or before circle time, for example. The picture opposite shows one example of a classroom pledge developed by Grade 4 students.

Understanding of the rules

Before implementing these rules, the teacher needs to make sure that children understand the rules, giving them enough time to assimilate them in order to guarantee that they can put them into practice when required. When children follow class rules, it is important to appreciate their efforts and praise them for it. This is a much better approach than waiting to catch them breaking the rules and then punishing them. If we praise children for good behaviour, this will boost their self-esteem and they will feel good about themselves.

When children break a class rule, the teacher's main concern shouldn't only be applying consequences. In fact, some children's misbehaviour is a genuine opportunity for learning. For example, in the case of a child bullying a classmate, the teacher needs to spend enough time looking into the problem, then guiding and helping the children to better manage themselves and their relationship with each other. These are valuable authentic learning opportunities that can be utilized to develop children's emotional intelligence.

Teachers need to have clear consequences for misbehaving or not following class rules; however, they should implement these with love, preserving the dignity of the child. It is important for the children to understand that it is their behaviour that is not acceptable and not them personally.

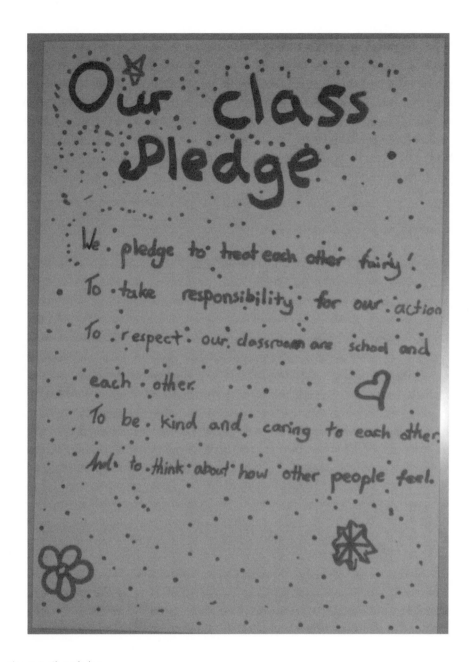

Figure 1: Class pledge

Developing class routines

Children love routine. Teachers need to have clear routines and work with the children to stick to them. When introducing any change to class routines, we must communicate them to the children. Children feel safe when they know exactly what the teacher expects them to do. They also feel good about themselves when they feel that their teacher is happy with them. A teacher's smile or a simple gesture of satisfaction means a lot to young children.

Giving children choices

Some children feel stressed out when they face tasks that are beyond their current ability, and this can have a negative effect on their well-being and their achievements in school, as we will see in Chapter 5. We all know that there is diversity among learners. Children have multiple intelligences; they have different learning styles, different interests and different backgrounds and experiences. They also have different moods at different times of their school day. Giving children choice in terms of their approach to learning or the kind of activities they need to carry out can make them emotionally more settled and will contribute towards a smoother learning process and better learning outcomes.

When children feel a sense of achievement and success we see them smiling with joy, sometimes they even jump up trying to reach the sky with a piece of paper that carries a good grade or a positive inspiring comment. As the saying goes, 'nothing succeeds like success'.

Choosing to make a difference

As teachers, we are very lucky to be in a position to make a difference in the lives of the children we teach. The classroom is like a theatre and teachers are the directors. Teachers have a great influence on how children feel, think, act and learn. At the end of the show, children can leave the theatre with a big smile of achievement feeling proud of who they are. Or they can come down from the stage with a bitter feeling of failure, their heads down and avoiding eye contact. Robin Sharma in his book *The Monk Who Sold his Ferrari* (1999: 82) says 'If I have seen further than others, it is simply because I have stood on the shoulders of great teachers'. We all can choose to be giant teachers who can make a big difference in the lives of the little ones in our care.

Putting it into practice

Take small steps to create a positive learning environment for the children in your class. Here are some activities that can contribute to creating an emotionally intelligent learning environment:

It is all about us

This activity helps the children feel the ownership of their classroom. It also develops their sense of security since they will have the opportunity to use their space in class to present things, items or concepts that are important to them. As a teacher you can do the following:

1. Create a personal space for yourself – you may choose a display board or a corner of the classroom.
2. Decorate it with pictures of yourself, pictures of your family members, friends, or a famous person who inspired you. Children really enjoy it if you post a picture of yourself when you were the same age as the students are. You can also add your favourite quotes or sayings you believe in. Also, include items such as ticket stubs, a favourite scarf, or a book that has special meaning for you. Make this a beautiful personalized area, describing yourself and what is important to you.
3. Use this area as an example for the children to create their own personalized areas, decorated with pictures and objects that are important to them.
4. Once the personal areas or corners are ready, the teacher can invite the children to have a look around the room to get to know more about each other, or give them the opportunity to share what is important to them during class meetings. There is further discussion on class meetings in chapter 6.

We are all special

This activity aims at helping children to think more positively about their classmates and express their appreciation

1. You can invite the children to design friendship cards using coloured paper, pens and other decorative items.

2. The children then will choose a friend to address the card to, writing a positive point about their friend.

3. If you feel that the children cannot yet write full sentence, you can ask them to complete a sentence such as, 'I think you are special because . . .' or, 'I like you because . . .'. For very young children they can simply draw or you can scribe their responses.

4. In some classes there be will students who are not very popular. To avoid being in a situation where a child might feel left out, you can decide to do one of the following:
   • Write children's names on strips of paper and have children pick a name. They then write a positive point about that specific child
   • Each child will send a card to the child he is sitting beside
   • You can divide the class into small groups and they all send cards to each other. In this case, the group number should not exceed three to four children
   • You can ask the students to send the card to someone who they do not know very well in the class.

5. Once all cards all ready, share them among the children and they can be used to decorate the class.

Acts of kindness

This activity teaches the children to be empathetic and kind to each other. It also teaches them to develop better relationships with others and to be more reflective.

1. You can first explain to the children the importance of being kind to others and the different things that children can do to be kind to each other. You can relate kindness to empathy, where children look out for each other and work on understanding their friends' points of view or feelings.

2. Secondly, you can give examples of little acts of kindness such as listening to each other, sharing toys, or helping each other with homework.

3. Children then give appropriate help to each other when the need arises.

4. They can then reflect on the experience and write their feelings in their journals or discuss acts with the class during class meetings. You can also create a display board to celebrate acts of kindness by allowing the students to post things they have done to help others and how they felt about it or kind acts of which they have been the recipient.

No bully zone

A disturbing event for children and one that creates a negative classroom environment is bullying. The activity below develops children's awareness towards the negative effects of bullying and can contribute to helping children to be more empathic and enhancing better relationships between children in the class.

1. The teacher discusses with the class the importance of having a classroom where everyone feels safe, respected and happy. She also discusses the negative effects of being a bully or bullying others.

2. In groups students brainstorm what they can do to ensure that their class is a Bully Free Zone

3. Each group selects the three most important ideas and produces signs and posters to represent their ideas. Use the cards to make inspiring displays in the classroom or hallways.

4. As a variation, after brainstorming, each group can choose the most important ideas to them, write a sketch and then act it out.

Teacher reflection

When I first started out teaching, I didn't realize the importance of the environment. I was too busy trying to organize the curriculum and fit in all the many units that had to be completed. Only as I have read more and grown as a teacher have I realized that many classroom activities can be based around social emotional learning with a little extra effort. This in turn helps make the class a wonderful learning ground not only for the facts in books but of life experience as well.

Year 4 teacher

EQ theory link

Creating a positive learning environment is a prerequisite for developing children's EQ, without which a great deal of teacher effort will be wasted. These activities aim at developing children's self-awareness, self-expression, relationship management and being more empathic.

Recommended reading

Beane, A. (1990) *The Bully Free Classroom*. Minneapolis, MN: Free Spirit.
Fiske, E. (1991) *Smart Schools, Smart Kids*. New York: Simon and Schuster.
Kohn, A. (1999) *The Schools Our Children Deserve*. New York: Houghton Mifflin.
Mackenzie, R. (1996) *Setting Limits in the Classroom*. Rockland, CA: Prima.
Wood, G. (1992) *Schools That Work*. New York: Penguin.

Reflective questions

1. Reflect on your class or context. What could you do to create a positive learning environment for the children you teach?

2. What are the most challenging things you might face in creating such an environment?

3. If you have any challenges, how can you overcome them?

4. Do you need any kind of support from your school administration? If so, clarify what help you need. How are you going to resolve the situation?

5. Do you need support from the parents of the children you teach? If so, please specify. What will you do to obtain the help you need?

4 Setting the Stage for Learning

Identifying feelings

> When dealing with people, remember you are not dealing with creatures of logic, but creatures of emotions.
>
> Dale Carnegie

> It is nearly impossible to teach a kid who is not ready to learn.
>
> Dennis Littky

> The biggest single problem of our profession is that we never learned how to deal with emotion in school.
>
> Robert Sylvester

A note to Carl's parents

Jimmy and Carl recently became friends when Jimmy and his family moved next door. They care about each other a great deal and look out for each other in difficult situations. Carl is rather a shy boy and he stutters when he feels embarrassed or tense.

Carl's schoolmates had noticed his stutter and were starting to pick on him. They would tease him by mimicking him, often provoking an angry response. In the past, the teasing had occasionally resulted in a physical fight. Since Jimmy became a constant presence by Carl's side, the fighting has ceased; Jimmy is big and tough.

One day, Carl was playing with a boy named Adam from another class. At first, everything was fine, and then all of a sudden children were running from all corners to watch a fight. Jimmy was absent from school that day and so Carl was left to defend himself. Some children from his class came running to help, but they couldn't do much because older kids from higher grades who were trying to separate the two children surrounded Carl. Luckily, Carl was not hurt, but he was feeling very unhappy and frustrated. He sat in a corner feeling annoyed. After recess was over the children went back to class.

The teacher, Mrs Johnson, knew that something had happened as soon as the children came into the classroom. Some of the children seemed upset and mumbled as they came into the room. A couple of children wanted to tell her what had happened, but she didn't listen. She sent them back to their desks and started her lesson.

She continually had to ask the children to concentrate and pay attention. Mrs Johnson had to repeat instructions several times. Towards the end of the lesson, she asked the class to open their books and do some exercises.

While going round to check their answers she was furious to see that a lot of the children hadn't done very much work. She went to check Carl's work. He hadn't done anything. He had been doodling all over the page. She chastised him and told him to finish the work at home. She then wrote a note to his parents in his diary saying:

> Dear Parent,
>
> Carl didn't pay attention in class today. He wasted his time doodling all over his book and didn't finish his class work. Please finish it with him as homework.
>
> Sincerely,
>
> Mrs Johnson

In everyday school life, children go through many emotional difficulties. For some children their emotional life can become unstable or they might start to feel insecure. This can lead to a serious negative impact not only upon the learning process but also upon their life in general.

We must not ignore emotions as we know they are very powerful. Ellison (2001: 7) states 'Emotions arouse our attention; they are at the core of our survival mechanisms.' Greenspan (1997) writes that emotions 'create, organize and orchestrate many of the mind's most important functions'.

Since we know emotions have such a powerful effect upon children's learning and general well-being, we must teach children how to develop their emotional intelligence. Goleman (1995) informs us that 'Emotional intelligence, unlike IQ, is not fixed at birth. On the contrary it can, and should, be taught.'

The first building block of emotional intelligence is self-awareness. This is the foundation of all other emotional intelligence skills. Goleman (1995: 51) says 'This awareness of emotions is the fundamental emotional competence on which others, such as emotional self-control, build.'

Self-awareness means recognizing feelings as they occur. Children need to learn how to recognize their feelings, name them and talk about them. They also need to learn the different strategies that will enable them to handle their emotional distress in a positive way. Children are not born with these skills; they need significant practice to develop them. Ellison (2001) advises 'All children need practice in handling their emotions, because it is a developmental issue'.

In this chapter, we shall look at the different tools and strategies that you can use to develop children's self-awareness. We shall focus on identifying feelings, naming them and talking about them.

Putting it into practice

The feeling thermometer

The feeling thermometer is a tool that children can use to measure their emotional temperature. The design is similar to an ordinary thermometer but in a child-friendly application. A scale of one to ten is marked on the thermometer. One represents mild feelings whereas ten shows extremely strong feelings.

1. Prepare a thermometer for each child with laminated faces representing three main emotions: happiness, sadness, anger. Prepare a fourth, blank face, to represent other emotions that the children wish to express. They can write or draw the expressions they feel on the face.

2. Display the thermometers on a bulletin board at child height. You can also include a title such as 'How Do I Feel Today?' or 'My Feeling Thermometer' as seen in the photo below. Put the different faces and the child's name above or under each thermometer.

3. If you want to use the feeling thermometer at the beginning of the year when you do not yet know the children's names, you may ask them to colour their thermometers and write their names above or below, in order to reinforce their sense of ownership of the instrument.

How to use the feeling thermometer in class

The feeling thermometer can be used in different ways. Use the thermometer to gauge a child's feelings at a particular point in time and to develop his self-awareness. For example, the teacher might be concerned about a child who appears preoccupied with a problem. She might have noticed that this child is not as happy or as active as he was. The feeling thermometer can be used to help the child reflect on how he is

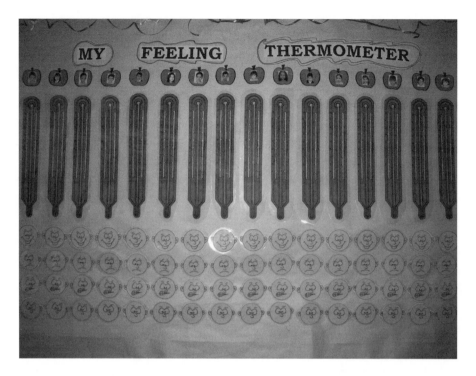

Figure 2: EQ thermometer board

feeling, to identify how he feels and to give this feeling an expression or a name by choosing the face that represents it. Children can quantify the strength of their feeling or emotion by using a scale from one to ten. The whole process leads the child to a development of his own self-awareness. The next step would be to help the child to express his emotions and thoughts and to help him learn how to handle his distressed emotions in a positive way. You can do this in many different ways, as we shall discuss in later chapters of the book.

Another way of using the feeling thermometer is for you to measure the general feeling or emotional temperature of the class to see how ready they are to learn and to give the children the chance to express their emotions if they want to. For example, after recess, the children come to class and you sense that something had happened that seems to be bothering them. You know from their body language and facial expressions that they are not at their best, that something is wrong. You can ask the whole class to show their emotional temperature. In a couple of minutes, all emotions will be on the feeling board. You can tell at a glance the emotional temperature of your class. If it is high then you need to think about utilizing activities aimed at reducing stress (see Chapter 5 on stress relief). Once the children feel more relaxed, the learning process will be more effective and you will be able to work towards a better learning outcome.

My special bag

This activity aims at helping the children to be aware of what is important to them and to develop their relationships with others by finding common interests. The underlying concept is to help them discover their own values. As a teacher, you can be a model for the children in your class.

1. Decorate a bag creatively with your name on it.
2. Put in the bag things that are special to you. For example, a family photo, your favourite story/ book, something to represent your hobby, like a tennis ball, a special gift, or a toy you have treasured.
3. Share the content of your bag with the children in circle time, talking about the items, explaining why they are special to you and how they make you feel.
4. Ask the children to do the same. They can decorate the bag in class and take it home to fill with things that are special to them.

Paper plate mask

This activity helps the children to get in touch with their feelings, recognizing what makes them happy, sad or angry.

1. Ask each child to make three paper plate masks, representing three emotions; for younger children, use happiness, sadness and anger but older children may wish to use emotions that are more complex.
2. In groups, the children talk about what made them feel each of the emotions they chose to display. They can also tell stories about things that happened to them to represent that feeling.
3. During class meeting time, each child chooses one of his masks and shares his feelings or his story.

Teacher reflection

As a teacher, I realized that we come to class and faithfully do our job. We do not notice how some children who are noisy are actually calling for attention, etc. As time is short and we have to complete the curriculum we do tend to overlook the reasons behind such behaviour. I used the feeling thermometer to find out how the children felt in my class. I used it to check their general emotional state when I felt that there was a negative feeling among the children. I also used it with individual children when I was not sure about their emotions. The results were astonishing; the thermometers told me a lot about my children's feelings.

Year 2 teacher

Recommended reading

Elias, M.J., Zins, J.E., Weisberg, R.P., Frey, K.S., Greenberg, M.T. and Haynes, N.M. (1997) *Promoting Social and Emotional Learning: Guidelines for Educators*. Alexandria, VA: Association for Supervision and Curriculum Development.

Freedman, J., Jensen, A., Ridcout, M. and Freedman, P. (2001) *Handle with Care, Emotional Intelligence Activity Book* (2nd Edn). San Mateo, CA: Six Seconds.

Noddings, N. (1992) *The Challenge to Care in Schools: An Alternative Approach to Education*. New York: Teachers College Press.

Palmer, P. (1998) *The Courage to Teach*. San Francisco: Jossey-Bass.

Rae, T. (1998) *Dealing with Feeling*. London: Paul Chapman.

Reflective questions

1. Is identifying children's emotions important to you? Why/why not?

2. What do you think about the idea of checking children's emotional temperature? In what situations would you do this?

3. Can you think of any other ways of checking children's emotional temperature?

4. What would you do if the class as whole seemed to be emotionally unhappy or upset?

5. What would you do if you noticed negative emotions among the children you teach?

5

Stress Relief

Don't underestimate the value of doing nothing, of just going along, listening to all the things you can't hear and not bothering.

Pooh's Little Instruction Book, inspired by A. A. Milne

Sometimes it's important to work for that pot of gold. But other times it's essential to take time off and to make sure that your most important decision in the day simply consists of choosing which colour to slide down on the rainbow.

Douglas Pages

The greatest weapon against stress is our ability to choose one thought over another.

William James

Alison's stressful childhood

Alison is a child under a great deal of stress. She is unpopular at school and often spends breaktime playing alone. Occasionally, she makes a friend, but it usually only lasts for a day or two before the other child moves on to someone else. Ten-year-old Alison faces a great deal of stress at home too. She lives alone with her mother and her younger brother. Her father left home when she was two and she has no further contact with him. She is often alone and needs to care for her baby brother while her mother does odd jobs to bring in more income.

Alison alleviates her stress by doing several things: watching television, fighting with other children, or seeking attention from adults. She usually stays up late at night, causing her to have a further of lack concentration in class the next day and to become even more temperamental.

Alison's teacher doesn't see the stress in her students' lives. She is so involved with completing the curriculum and getting by each day that she doesn't seem to notice Alison's troubles. In fact, she sees her as a disruptive, somewhat annoying child in the class who causes the class to get off track at times. Alison is in great need of a caring adult to show her productive and useful ways of dealing with her stress.

Luckily, a student teacher visiting the school, Ms White, took a great interest in Alison. The positive attention from this teacher allowed Alison to open up and share some of the problems she had encountered. Together Ms White and Alison made a stress-relief plan for her to follow. Alison began writing in her journal daily about how she was feeling and she carried a card listing several options she could take when she was feeling angry or bored so she could refer to it at times when her mind was not clear. Over the six-week period with Ms White, Alison began to gain confidence. Ms White had spoken with her mother and an earlier bedtime was enforced. Ms White had given Alison books to read such as *Stick up for Yourself* by Kaufman, Raphael and Esplenad (1999). Without help, Alison might have faced a downward spiral of unhappiness and unsociability. Due to the help of one teacher who cared, Alison blossomed and found a way to improve her behaviour and actions, learnt how to make friends and to improve her stress levels. Even one teacher can make a huge difference to one child. Let's all strive to be that teacher, the one who children remember for years to come, the one who made a difference in their lives.

Stress and its effect on learning

Countless children are subject to school-related stressors such as low grades, overly challenging classroom settings, athletic requirements, peer relationships, exams and clashes with teachers (Jewett, 1997). Although occasional or moderate stress is for the most part healthy, being exposed to high stress levels over time can damage and impair children's cognition (Jensen, 2005). When the mind experiences high stress, learning cannot take place. In fact, some children can feel emotionally hijacked when they have an argument with a friend, receive disappointing marks or don't understand lessons. Goleman (1995) explores the idea of 'emotional hijacking'. He stated 'the hijacking occurs in an instant, triggering this reaction crucial moments before the neocortex, the thinking brain, has a chance to glimpse fully at what is happening, let alone decide if it is a good idea'. Of course, this is of concern in education. In fact, Harvard professor Jack Shonkoff (2007) informs us that 'When faced with a potentially threatening situation, like the first day at a new school, a child needs to find a way to cope. However, not all stress is equal in its ability to cause havoc to our brains. Research shows that excessive experience with toxic stress can disrupt the development of brain circuits related to stress response – and to learning and memory.'

Stress-relief activities

We recommend starting your class each day with some forms of stress-relief activities. Several practical meditation activities are included in this chapter. We will introduce other activities such as the 'dumping bin' where children write negative or angry feelings on a strip of paper and then throw them away. However, before that we need to teach children to recognize when they are feeling stress and to help them recognize when others are feeling stress. We can do this through discussion with the children about facial expressions, feelings in their stomachs, etc. When you feel stressed yourself, tell the children and ask them if they saw any physical signs in you.

Dr Cooper (1996) mentions that 'If we lack emotional intelligence, whenever stress rises the human brain switches to autopilot and has an inherent tendency to do more of the same, only harder which, more often than not, is precisely the wrong approach in today's world.'

The brain has a short pathway from the thalamus to the amygdale that guarantees that we respond rapidly to emotionally valid information. Think back on your own education and childhood – our strongest memories link with strong emotions (Le-Doux, 1996).

The gift of de-stressing

De-stressing can be an important part of classroom routines. As research shows that learning cannot take place when the brain is preoccupied, it is important to allow children to clear their minds and become more in tune with their own feelings and emotions. A trigger of stress can be by something as simple as arriving to find a substitute teacher in the classroom or realizing that they left their homework at home. One of the best gifts you can give a child is teaching them how to manage their own stress levels; they will take this with them throughout their lives. In fact, too many children do not have good role models on how to deal with stress. Many adults never learnt how to manage their stress and therefore manage it by tuning out and watching TV, shouting at family members, or eating or drinking. John Gottman (1997) states:

In the last decade or so, science has discovered a tremendous amount about the role emotions play in our lives. Researchers have found that, even more than IQ, your emotional awareness and abilities to handle feelings will determine your success and happiness in all walks of life, including family relationships.

Putting it into practice

Meditation exercises

Meditation provides you with a way to cool down and bring the children in your class into focus. Meditation helps children clear their minds, get ready for learning and have better concentration. Perfect for after PE lessons or break times, this simple method allows children to calm their bodies and minds and relax.

1. Children can do these activities at desks or they may prefer to lie down on the floor or get into a more comfortable position.
2. Ask children to close their eyes. Ask them to imagine they are in another place where they feel calm and happy.
3. Ask the children to breathe in deeply. Breathe in. Breathe out. Continue deep breathing for one minute. It is a good idea to play soft classical music or nature sounds in the background.
4. Begin to read the meditation exercises in a slow, even voice, taking time between the words or phrases.
5. At the end of the meditation, you may wish to continue with the deep breathing.
6. Ask children to open their eyes. Stand up slowly, stretch their arms and notice how relaxed they feel.

Meditation 1

Close your eyes ... breathe in deeply ... relax your body ... imagine a warm, rainy day ... listen to the raindrops dripping slowly and magically from the sky ... Breathe in and look at the clouds above ... see the sunshine peeking out from behind ... feel the calmness of the day ... imagine a rainbow in the sky ... see the colours of the rainbow ... see how it sparkles and shines ... imagine yourself climbing the rainbow reaching for your dreams ... reaching and reaching to the clear blue sky until you can grab your dreams in your arms.

Meditation 2

Relax . . . close your eyes . . . imagine you are a star shining brightly in the night sky . . . breathe in deeply . . . breathe out all your negative energy . . . for you are a free star shining in the dark sky . . . breathe in . . . imagine yourself flying around visiting all the other stars or floating higher and higher . . . in the sky peacefully . . . breathe out again . . . and breathe in deeply full of hopes and dreams from the night sky. . . and finally breathe out.

Meditation 3

Breathe in deeply . . . relax your arms . . . relax your legs . . . let your neck and your face release all the tension inside . . . breathe out all the stress that has built up in your body . . . let your feet hang peacefully . . . loosen your shoulders . . . feel all the tension being released as you breathe deeply out of your stomach . . . imagine your body is calm and relaxed . . . imagine you are floating . . . all the weight has been removed from your body . . . you are weightless and free . . . feel your calm, relaxed body swaying in the wind and feeling happy and light-hearted . . . breathe in and breathe out . . . allow your mind to imagine a state of calm and happiness . . . slowly open your eyes . . .

Deep breathing

This simple exercise is very rewarding. Simply by teaching children to breathe in and out deeply they can release some of the pent-up stress in their systems. Try it yourself! Starting a class with 10 deep breaths in and out can work wonders! It is also a great strategy to teach during anger management. By breathing in a controlled fashion, children take the time to think about their actions before they speak or act angrily with another person.

1. Explain the benefits of deep breathing to your children. Perhaps they can brainstorm with you or do a search on the internet to find ideas.
2. Model the deep breathing method to the children in your class by breathing in deeply and releasing your breath. Repeat several times.
3. Invite the children to breathe in with you and breathe out. Repeat 10 to 12 times.

The throw away

The Throw Away is a favourite activity from our classrooms. This activity allows children to express their thoughts in writing and to get rid of them by crumpling them up and throwing them away.

1. Give children strips of coloured paper.
2. Children write down any angry or disturbing thought or feeling and/or can simply scribble on the paper.
3. Children then tear up the paper, crumple it and throw it away in a rubbish bin. Items written down may be private, or children may wish to share them during class meetings or circle time.
4. Explain to children that sometimes writing down a negative thought can release the negativity than is built up in their system.

EQ theory link

Stress-relief activities come under the self-awareness and self-management categories in the framework. Children become more aware of when they are feeling stress and are able to use the tools they have to relieve some of that stress, thus managing their feelings before they feel out of control.

Teacher reflection

Meditation has changed the way our students act considerably! We implemented morning meditation sessions in our classrooms during homeroom time and found that the students calmed down and focused more in their lessons. Several students also indicated that it helped them to do the exercise before their exams as a way to feel calm and collected.

Year 3 teacher

Recommended reading

Belknap, M. (1996) *Stress Relief for Kids: Taming Your Dragons*. New York: Whole Person Associates.

Dupont, C. and Dupont, M. (2003) *The Anxiety Cure for Kids: A Guide for Parents*. Hoboken, NJ: John Wiley.

Eastman, M. and Rozen, S. (1994) *Taming the Dragon in Your Child*. Hoboken, NJ: John Wiley.

Garth, M. (1993) *Moonbeam: A Book of Meditations for Children*. San Francisco: Harper.

Huebner, D. (1995) *What to Do When You Worry Too Much: A Kid's Guide to Overcoming Anxiety (What to Do Guides for Kids)*. Washington DC: Magination Press.

Sorensen, E. (1993) *Children's Stress and Coping: A Family Perspective*. New York: Guilford Press.

Wilde, J. (1997) *Hot Stuff to Help Kids Chill Out*. Richmond, IN: Lgr.

Williams, M. (2005), *Cool Cats, Calm Kids*. Alascadero, CA: Impact.

Reflective questions

1. Is your classroom stress free?

2. Do you gauge the stress level of the children in your class before you start?

3. Do you equip the children with tools to de-stress themselves?

4. What activities can you introduce to help children manage their stress levels?

5. Can you think back to a time when a child in your class was experiencing a high level of stress? What would you do differently now?

6

Class Meetings

Even beyond the interpersonal area, class meeting time is valuable for children's learning and cognitive development.

Vance Weaver

The way a child learns how to make decisions is by making decisions not by following directions.

Alfie Kohn

If I can make a difference in one child's life, it makes the whole year worth it!

Tasneem K. Nabee

Somebody ripped my painting!

Alex's face crumpled up in a frown. He sat alone in the corner. Tears started to well up in his eyes. 'What happened?' asked Sarah, a bright little girl with a kind heart.

'Somebody ripped my painting' cried Alex. Sarah looked and saw the bright-coloured painting of a fire truck with a big hole in the centre. Sarah told Mrs Wade their teacher. 'Somebody ripped Alex's painting; I think we should hold a class meeting.'

After break, all the children sat in a circle. Mrs Wade asked Alex to explain what had happened. Tearfully, he held up his ripped painting and said he had found it this way after hanging it up to dry in the art corner.

'I know who did it' shouted Katelyn. 'Well,' said Mrs Wade, 'if that person would like to tell us we will let them say so themselves. For now, though let's try to solve the problem. Does anybody have any suggestions?' 'He could tape it together again', volunteered Lisa. 'Or he could just say "Never mind"', said Michael. 'No,' said, Alex, 'that wouldn't be OK because I was going to give my mom the painting for Mother's Day' 'Excuse me, Mrs Wade,' a teary-eyed Salman called out, 'it was me! I did it. I didn't mean to – it was an accident, but I thought I would get into trouble so I put the picture back. I want to help Alex paint a new picture. I could get the paints ready and wash the brushes.' 'What do you think Alex?' asked Mrs Wade. 'That sounds good', he smiled. 'At least I can still give my mum her painting!' 'Does anyone else want to say anything?' 'There you are – it's better to own up if you make a mistake. Then the problem can be solved.' said Mrs Wade, wrapping up the class meeting.

During school hours, children go through various issues that might affect them emotionally. They get so preoccupied with these feelings that the learning channel becomes blocked. 'Learning doesn't take place in isolation from kids' feelings. Being emotionally literate is as important for learning as instruction in math and reading' (Goleman, 1995: 301). Sylwester (1998) strongly suggests that children need help to become emotionally literate. Many schools are seriously deficient in this area. 'The biggest single problem of our profession is that we never learned how to deal with emotion in school' (Sylwester 1998:25).

Ellison (2001: 22) urges schools to take on the responsibility for the emotional development and well being of the child, emphasizing that it is an obligation and not a choice 'For many children our schools play a major role in teaching them how to handle their emotions. It is not a question of whether or not we want to take on this responsibility. We must take the responsibility.'

Taking the responsibility to develop a child's EQ might not always be an easy task, but ignoring the issue can have negative consequences. In addition, a child who does learn how to be emotionally intelligent will most likely have a much improved school experience than a child who was not taught these skills.

What is the responsibility of educators in coaching children to settle conflicts calmly, instead of using intimidation or threats of violence? We must present children with opportunities to experience caring environments, challenge injustice, engage in decision-making, observe pro-social behaviour modelled by adults and develop conflict resolution skills (Carlsson-Paige and Lantieri, 2005).

To facilitate the development of a child's EQ, you need to provide them with an appropriate set of strategies that will enable them to get the results they work so hard to achieve. The use of class meetings or circle time is one such strategy.

What is a class meeting?

Class meetings are an ideal way to let children become engaged in productive decision-making in their classrooms. Children develop feelings of respect, trust and appreciation among teachers and other children. Class meetings assist children in creating their own systems of accountability and responsibility for their classroom.

If we give children the opportunity to develop these systems themselves a better sense of responsibility results as they have ownership over the process. Children feel more motivated and positive towards the school when they believe they have a say in the processes.

Class meetings are an effective way for children to reflect on their practices, express themselves, listen to each other, be empathetic and develop their problem-solving skills. We can discuss in a positive way the daily situations that arise in school and the children themselves can reflect on their behaviour and come up with feasible solutions to the problems they encounter.

A class meeting can take place during a regularly allotted time for such discussions. The first or last 15 minutes of class may be appropriate or simply a time when you or a child in the class thinks it is necessary. One way to implement this is to have a box in the class where children can fill in a slip indicating their desire for a meeting and what they want to discuss. These slips can be anonymous or children can identify themselves depending on how comfortable they are.

We recommend setting up a class meeting in a way that is caring, friendly and emotionally safe. The size of the group should be reasonable. If the number is too large, the meeting will not be effective, as not all children will have the opportunity to express their feelings or points of view. With larger numbers, too, the task of reaching a solution that satisfies everyone becomes more difficult. With a reasonably sized group, the children will feel more connected and the bond between them will grow faster. In larger classes, it may be advisable to break the class into two smaller groups.

Putting it into practice

Talking stick

Native American Indians have utilized the talking stick for hundreds of years as a way to have a fair and impartial discussion. The use of the talking stick was to authorize who had the privilege of speaking during community meetings. When difficult problems arose, the principal elder would hold the talking stick and embark on the debate. When he completed his point of view he would offer the talking stick to the group and anyone who wanted to speak after him would take it. The Native American Indians would pass the stick around until all parties had a chance to express their point of view and come to a joint solution in a civil and organized manner.

Explain the tradition to the children and ask a group of children to make a 'talking stick for the class to use during class meetings'. Once a meeting has been decided as part of a regular timeslot or at the request of yourself or the children due to an issue that has arisen, join in a circle. The children will need to feel that you are not preoccupied and able to focus so that they can open up, so make sure you are in the correct frame of mind. Use your own emotional intelligence skills to check your own emotional state and be prepared to adjust it if necessary. Alternatively, if this is not possible, you might want to postpone this meeting to another more suitable time. Holding the talking stick give a brief introduction to clarify the purpose of the meeting. If the aim of the meeting is to rectify a specific situation, encourage the children concerned to speak up first each taking turns to hold the stick. Listen actively and avoid being judgemental. Acknowledge problems. Acknowledging doesn't mean that you agree with what they say; it simply means that you understand the problem from their point of view and realize how they feel about it. Try not to give ready answers or solutions. Help the children reach an agreement and solve their own problems. Appreciate their honesty and thank them for it. Make sure, as far as possible, that everyone leaves in a happy frame of mind.

Small-group/specific-issue meetings

We suggest this approach when you want to develop specific skills in a small group of children or when there is a problem or an issue to be resolved with a small group. For example, a small group of children are bullying a child who is new to the class. You as the class teacher find this unacceptable. You hold a class meeting and share your observations and perceptions with the children. You invite all the children including the child who was bullied to express their points of view and how they feel about it. You listen to everyone, give everyone the chance to speak until the children resolve the issue among themselves. You can facilitate the discussion on emotions at the beginning by providing faces with different emotions on it. You can ask children to show the emotion they feel about the situation and then discuss it.

Figure 3: Group discussion with the help of emotion cue cards.

Teacher reflection

Class meetings helped my classroom to flourish. Children became responsible for their own behaviour management and helped each other to find solutions to problems in creative and caring ways. Starting your day with a morning class meeting provides numerous opportunities to support social and emotional learning: It helps build a sense of community, creates a climate of trust, encourages respectful communication and much, much more.

Year 5 teacher

EQ theory link

Class meeting time develops self-awareness and relationship management skills in children. By discovering the consequences their actions have on the feelings of others, children are able to develop empathy and respect for others. Children hear other people's stories and are able to see how that person feels – a perspective they may have been unable to visualize previously.

Recommended reading

Borba, M. and Craig B. (1993) *Self-Esteem: A Classroom Affair, 101 Ways to Help Children like Themselves*. San Francisco: Harper.

Curwin, R. L. and Mendler, N. A. (1998) *Discipline with Dignity*. Alexandria, VA: Association for Supervision and Curriculum Development.

Dreikurs, R. and Loren G. (1993) *New Approach to Discipline: Logical Consequences*. New York: Plume.

Gootman, M. E. (2000) *The Loving Parents' Guide to Discipline: How to Teach Your Child to Behave – With Kindness, Understanding, and Respect*. New York: Berkeley.

Kreidler, W. J. and Tsubokawa, S. (1999) *Early Childhood Adventures in Peacemaking: A Conflict Resolution Guide for Early Childhood Educators* (2nd edn). Cambridge, MA: Educators for Social Responsibility.

Styles, D. (2001) *Class Meetings*. Markham, ON: Pembroke.

Sullo, R. (1993) *Teach Them to be Happy*. Chapel Hill, NC: New View.

Reflective questions

1. Have you ever used the class meeting in your teaching experience? How did you find it?

2. Do you think using class meetings would be useful in your context? If yes, please justify.

3. Would class size be an issue? If yes, how can you solve this problem?

4. What are the characteristics of effective class meetings?

5. Do you think you might face obstacles in implementing class meetings? If so, what kind(s) of obstacles, and how can you overcome them?

6. What benefits do you think you and you class will gain from implementing class meetings?

7 Journal Writing

I love writing. I love the swirl and swing of words as they tangle with human emotions.

James Michener

Writing, I think, is not apart from living. Writing is a kind of double living. The writer experiences everything twice. Once in reality and once in that mirror which waits always before or behind.

Catherine Drinker Bowen, *Atlantic*, December 1957

Journal writing is its own reward. Once you get started, your journal will become another one of your good friends – one who is always available and has the time to listen attentively.

Unknown

When seeking to increase the ability of children to assume another's perspective, it is most fruitful to have them focus first on their own feelings – the different kinds of feelings they have and what feelings are associated with what kinds of situations.

Black and Phillips 1982

Ahmed's powerful words

Ahmed had the worst day ever. At least he thought it was. He ran to his room and slammed the door shut. He pulled his journal from under his desk. First, he had forgotten his homework. He had really done it and he had worked hard on it too, but Ms Jones has just deplored 'No excuses!' and he got a zero. Then his friend Billy got a new Power Ranger toy but instead of letting him play with him, he went off with Troy who had one too, and they said he couldn't play until he brought a Power

Ranger as well. He was all alone in the break and he could feel his chest tightening and his throat starting to ache.

At least he had English next, he loved Ms Smart, she always smiled at him and he knew that she liked him even if he forgot his homework sometimes. Last month everyone had started writing a journal. The journal was secret and only Ms Smart and each child could see it. They could write anything they liked in it but Ms Smart asked them to write about their feelings and how they solved problems. She had taught them to go back and read days when they were sad or angry, to see if their solution had worked, how they felt about it now and if it was really as big a deal as they had thought at the time.

Ahmed remembered another day when Billy hadn't played with him; he thought Billy would never play with him again. He had written about how sad he was and that he would be alone every break time from then on. But as Ahmed read the pages in-between he realized that that wasn't true. They had played together every other day apart from today again. Once Ahmed started writing he felt better, at least Ms Smart would know how he felt. Sometimes she even gave suggestions to them on how they could solve their problems. Once a week Ms Smart had 'conference time' together with her students one by one and she would ask them to think of solutions to their problems.

Ahmed felt better after he wrote about his anger and sadness. As he read back from days gone by he realized that this was just a bump in the road and that it would pass just as his other bad days had.

Learning about self through journal writing

Journal writing is a wonderful way of expressing emotions. With journal writing comes the skill of using emotional literacy. That is the ability to understand, express and recognize your emotions. At times we may not even be aware of our feelings and yet they influence us profoundly. By encouraging children to write in journals this self-awareness will be established.

Goleman (1995) explains how the brain is competing for learning and strong emotions to work in sync. Any experienced teacher can tell you the impact a negative event has on classroom learning. This is because the amygdala is hijacked and causes children to lose concentration on the learning at hand while they sort out their emotional base. By giving children a tool such as journal writing, they are able to work through their emotions in a positive manner.

Journal writing can help children by liberating internal stress. When we hold onto powerful emotions without truly expressing them, then inhibitions are created leading to internal stress on our minds and bodies. Journal writing can help children to integrate and understand their feelings and thoughts while experiencing a release of stress.

Writing about personal problems is known to help people by allowing for a release of the negative emotions surrounding the dilemma (Pennebaker, 1997). Coping with traumatic or stressful happenings through therapeutic writing has been deliberated at length over the last 15 years. Therapeutic writing entails writing about the emotions, feelings and views surrounding a stressful incident. Research shows that writing for short periods for several days in a row can lead to productive outcomes (Pennebaker and Seagal, 1999). In fact, benefits of writing to express emotions can include higher grades and fewer visits to medical practitioners (Pennebaker and Francis, 1996) and better self-awareness of personal issues (Francis and Pennebaker, 1991).

Putting it into practice

As part of encouraging children to write we must prepare them with the correct vocabulary and improve their emotional literacy. A list of words is included in the Emotional Literacy Bank in the Appendix. Depending on the age of the children in your class you can introduce these words by including an emotional literacy wall in your classroom. Introducing an emotional literacy word bank at the back of the child's journal where they can add words as they learn them or come across them, or by simply bringing up these words in daily lesson time as appropriate, is also a good idea.

You can have children write a feelings journal in which they document their emotional reactions to situations that occur in school such as their accomplishments, failures and interactions. Try to make journal writing a regular occurrence by providing time for it. Five to ten minutes at the start or end of a lesson are enough time for most kids to jot down their feelings and emotions. Developing journal writing into a daily habit is a gift children will cherish for a lifetime.

The design of the journal should be a personal choice and is very important. If children like the book, they are more likely to treasure it and to use it frequently. Children may like a ready-made book, or may prefer to choose a blank cover and decorate and design it themselves.

Dear Journal,

I feel sad, and bad
and relly, really **MAD!**
My mom is being really mean,
being really mad. Sometimes
I just want to cry.
My mom is always blames
me! When I didn't do a thing!
She always makes a scary
face with small creepy eyes.
like the time I got in
trubbile because My sister
spilt her milk!! I just
wantted to cry and shout.
Before my sister Emma
was born my parents never
got mad at me, they
always told me I was
the best and I always will
be. But now I'm the second
best. Sometimes I felt jealous
of Emma, but today I
just plain old **MAD!**

Figure 4: A child expressing anger and frustration

Using current events to stimulate thoughts

1. Bring in an article from a newspaper or a magazine about an issue they may be interested in and which would promote empathy and read it with the children. Topics such as war, natural disasters, or fundraising for illnesses make for good discussion points. In future, encourage the children to bring in the articles themselves.

2. Hold a discussion with the children on the topic. What emotions come up in the discussion: fear, disgust, jealousy, anger, sadness, or joy?

3. Children can then use their journals to write a response to the article. Other options you can explore include writing letters to the editors expressing their feelings on the topic. Work can also be done writing from the point of view of a person in the situation that is then discussed to promote empathy.

Emotional quotes

1. Give children a quote and ask them to respond in their journals. Discussion about the meaning of the quote will help to enhance this activity.

2. A list of suggested quotes is found below.

Emotional intelligence quotes to stimulate journal writing

Anger quotes

Anybody can become angry, that is easy; but to be angry with the right person and to the right degree, and at the right time, and for the right purpose, and in the right way, that is not within everybody's power, that is not easy.

Aristotle

He who angers you conquers you.

Elizabeth Kenny

Anger is one letter short of danger.

Unknown

People who fly into a rage always make a bad landing.

Will Rogers

Happy quotes

Success is not the key to happiness. Happiness is the key to success. If you love what you are doing, you will be successful.

Albert Schweitzer

To live happily is an inward power of the soul.

Aristotle

Happiness is not having what you want. It is wanting what you have.

Unknown

True happiness is not attained through self-gratification, but through fidelity to a worthy purpose.

Helen Keller

You will never be happier than you expect. To change your happiness, change your expectation.

Bette Davis

Envy, jealousy quotes

The grass is always greener on the other side

Unknown

Do not overrate what you have received, nor envy others. He who envies others does not obtain peace of mind

Prince Gautama Siddhartha

Using journals with small groups

1. Let the children read stories from the *Chicken Soup for the Soul* series, or other books with emotional stories. There are many interesting stories that children can relate to.

2. Have children try to put themselves in another person's shoes. For example, discuss what it must feel like to be a taxi driver on a hot summer's day, or a nurse in a rushed hospital. Think about a parent who has lost a child or mother who knows she is terminally ill. Ask the children to put themselves in those people's shoes and see if they can better understand their actions and emotions. This is one way of showing children how to develop empathy.

3. Children then write in their journals as though they are the person mentioned above.

4. Share the writings with the group and discuss why such thoughts and feelings emerged.

Using journal prompts

1. Write one of the prompts from the list below or your own on the board and ask children to complete their writing.

'I feel happiest when ...'

'The best day I ever had was ...'

'I feel sad when ...'

'I am most scared of . . .'

'Today I felt . . .'

'When I am angry I . . .'

'My greatest fear is . . .'

'My big goal is . . .'

'In the future, I hope to . . .'

'One thing I would like to improve in myself is . . .'

'My best qualities are . . .'

'One way I can be a better person would be to . . .'

'I feel lucky because . . .'

'I am grateful that . . .'

'If my friends ask me to do something I feel uncomfortable with, I would . . .'

'If I saw a friend being bullied, I would . . .'

'My idea to make our school bully-free is . . .'

'When I feel upset I . . .'

'When I feel envious I . . .'

EQ theory link

Self-awareness is developed by journal writing. Children are able to reflect and discover solutions for themselves through the art of writing. Journal writing not only helps with stress relief and providing a clearer vision for young children but it also helps them to reflect on their feelings. Children are able to reflect on their writings later in order to better understand the process of thinking and feeling they went through.

Teacher reflection

Journal writing has helped my students find a private place where they can safely express themselves without repercussions. They can say exactly what is on their mind and reflect on ways to solve their problems

Year 6 teacher

Recommended reading

Capacchione, L. (1989) *The Creative Journal for Children A Guide for Parents, Teachers and Counselors*. Cambria, CA: Shambhala.

Geiss, C. and Jessup, C. (2002). *Inner Outings: Adventures in Journal Writing*. Novato, CA: New World Library.

Meyer, L. (1997) *Quotes for Kids: Today's Interpretations of Timeless Quotes Designed to Nurture the Young Spirit*. Hershey, PA: Reach Press.

Perry, L. (2005) *Pictures of My Days – An Art and Writing Workbook for Creating the Life You Want*. East Cleveland, OH: Forest Hill.

Reflection questions

1. How can written expression help the children in your classroom?

2. Can your own written reflections help you to be a better teacher?

3. When completing language arts activities in your classroom can you integrate EQ into the task?

4. Do you encourage the children in your class to write their innermost thoughts and to review these thoughts at later dates?

8 Storytelling

If you don't know the trees you may be lost in the forest, but if you don't know the stories you may be lost in life.

Unknown

Life itself is the most wonderful fairytale of all.

Hans Christian Andersen

Storytelling is the most powerful way to put ideas into the world today.

Robert McKee

A new child in Mrs Lupton's class

Mrs Lupton's Year 5 class was busy preparing for their yearly play. All the parents were coming and there was lots of scurrying and running as the children prepared props and painted backgrounds. Everyone was in a festive mood, everyone apart from Sarah. Sarah's family had just moved to the neighbourhood and Sarah didn't have a part in the play because she had come too late. She felt awkward and in the way. Nobody spoke to her during break; she sat all alone. How she wished she were back in Canada at her old school. Instead, she was in a new country and a new school where everyone was too busy to notice her she thought. Although Mrs Lupton was a busy teacher, she was caring and she had noticed that Sarah was getting lost in all the action. Mrs Lupton invited everyone to sit in a circle – 'it's storytelling time' she announced, as she gathered the children around her. She had a carefully chosen book with her. As they read the story *Franklin's New Friend* (Bourgeois, 1997) about a new student who joins Franklin's class, she asked how the children thought that person would feel. She then asked the children what they could do since they had a new child in their class. Shyly some of the children looked at Sarah. 'We could invite her to play with us at break?' they said. 'We could let her help us with the play', said Tony. 'Hey, let's make a part for Sarah in the play', shouted Tommy. 'Yeah she could be a passerby on the road', said Melissa. 'What a good idea' exclaimed Ms Lupton. 'What do you think, Sarah?' She was very happy to be included. Maybe this place won't be so bad after all, she thought.

What is bibliotherapy?

Bibliotherapy, defined as the use of books to assist people in being able to solve problems, is a wonderful tool to develop emotional intelligence. Another, more precise definition is that bibliotherapy is a technique for structuring interaction between a facilitator and a participant based on the mutual sharing of literature (Pardeck, 1989).

Many children enter school without the required social, emotional and academic fundamentals needed in order to flourish. Books, stories and other literature or 'bibliotherapy' is one strategy that you can use to help individual children or small groups of children solve problems, develop empathy and cultivate further insight into themselves. Reading is a therapeutic device that enables us to relax, develop empathy for the characters in the book and take on roles we never would in real life. We frequently finish a book acquiring fresh perspectives and thoughts. By reading literature on a specific topic you can help children triumph over the emotional turbulences associated with real-life difficulties. These stories can then function as a catalyst for conversations and determination of potential solutions to predicaments children are facing. Storytelling encourages teachers to find books, stories or other reading materials corresponding to the distinct requirements of each child in order to support student attainment and improvement (Johnson, Wan, Templeton, Graham and Sattler, 2000). In fact, these stories and literature can serve as a springboard for intervention and self-regulation.

Bibliotherapy began long ago in ancient Greece where they used stories to cure those who were psychologically unwell (Stroud, Stroud and Staley, 1999). G. O. Ireland in 1930 was the first to suggest literature as a way of proposing resolutions to prevailing troubles and diminishing children's internal emotional unrest (Ouzts, 1991). In fact, Pardeck (1994) explains how counsellors 'prescribed' literature in the 1930s, after which librarians started to accumulate records of literature that could assist children in adjusting their views, emotions and behaviours.

The benefits of using storytelling in schools are obvious to most educators. While reading, children learn valuable lessons as they identify with a story's characters or predicaments. The more children can connect with a book's characters or storyline, the stronger the emotional bond they will experience. This connection lets children appreciate that others tackle comparable circumstances and situations, consequently affording a type of emotional healing (Herbert and Furner, 1997).

Objectives of bibliotherapy

Pardeck (1994) recognized bibliotherapy as having six potential objectives:

1. To offer information.
2. To provide insight into a specific experience or situation.
3. To provide alternative solutions to the problem.
4. To stimulate a discussion of what the actual problem is.
5. To communicate new values and attitudes with regard to the problem.
6. To help children understand that they are not the only one who has experienced this problem.

The guidelines below are to support the implementation of storytelling or bibliotherapy in the classroom.

1. Acknowledge the problem, circumstances, or difficulty to be resolved.
2. Choose a suitable book, story, or poem to share with a child or group of children.
3. Either read the story with the child or give the child the story to read alone.
4. Follow up with discussion and activities for the child(ren) in relation to the issues you wish to address.

Benefits for children

Goleman (1995) acknowledged six positive results from the use of bibliotherapy for children:

1. Fewer incidents of physical violence in the classroom.
2. Less name-calling.
3. Smaller numbers of put-downs.
4. Better conflict-resolution strategies.
5. Improved sensitivity towards fellow children.
6. Augmented capability of listening to classmates.

Putting it into practice

Storytelling allows children to identify and gain insight into their personality and to learn more about themselves and their responses to events or people. This self-awareness can facilitate a decrease in apprehension, despair and isolation experienced by numerous children with social or emotional problems. The ideas suggested below are a few ways you can help to improve EQ skills in the children you teach.

Small-group work

You notice that one of the children is feeling lonely. He does not seem to belong to any group, and during break time he spends most of his time wandering around aimlessly. Forcing him to join the other children is not a good idea, so you decide to develop the other children's awareness of the problem. The aim is to let them feel what this lonely child is going through and to encourage the children to choose to invite this child to be part of the group.

You choose a story that reflects the situation. We recommend *I'm Lonely (Your Feelings)* by Brian Moses (1997) for this particular situation.

1. Invite the children look at the cover of the book and read the title to predict what the storyline is.

2. Read the story aloud asking questions to check comprehension.

3. Focus the questions on the points that will help you achieve your target.

4. Ask the children to retell the story.

5. Let them reflect and talk about their own experiences and where appropriate ask them to imagine how the character of the story must have felt.

6. Relate the discussion to the current problem or concern if appropriate.

7. Let the children express their opinions and any solutions they may have for the characters.

8. Extension activities such as drawing, journal writing or drama can follow.

Individual difficulties

You know that Gemma, a child in kindergarten, is feeling upset as her parents have just divorced. In consultation with Gemma's parents, you as the teacher can offer Gemma a variety of books to read such as *Mama and Daddy Bear's Divorce* by Cornelia Maude Spelman (2001) or *Two Homes* by Claire Masurel (2001).

1. Select an appropriate book

2. Read aloud the story or involve the parents in reading the book to their child. If children are older they can read the book themselves.

3. Provide a time for discussion of the story and any similarities or differences to the characters they felt.

4. Follow up with expressive activities such as art, music or drama as described later in this book.

My point of view

1. Read the story *The True Story of the Three Little Pigs* by Jon Scieszka (1995). This chronicles the famous fairytale from the point of view of the wolf!

2. Discuss with the children our tendency to see things from one point of view, but explain that we must consider others' points of view as well.

3. Read children excerpts from books. Ask them to explain the point of view of the character. Then ask them to imagine they were the character's friend, mother, teacher or any other suitable character. How would that person feel?

4. In future, choose stories as needed but encourage children to step inside the character's shoes and imagine for a minute what that character was thinking and feeling. Think about how other characters feel as well.

5. Extension activities can include writing from two different points of view. For example, two children could each write a journal pretending to be different characters from the story. They can then share their journals with the class, discussing the emotions that each character felt and why.

EQ theory link

Storytelling can incorporate all five aspects of Goleman's framework. As they read and develop connections to stories, their own self-awareness is improved. Children can learn about empathy, management of emotions, and many other important traits from storytelling sessions that link to relationship awareness and management.

Teacher reflection

'I use stories regularly in my class. I try to find stories about bullying, different feelings and other situations that arise in my class. At times when I know one of my students is going through a personal event at home I provide them with specific reading material. I have seen the difference a story can make in a child's life and will always include stories in my classroom.

Year 3 teacher

Recommended reading

Kilpatrick, W. (1994) *Books That Build Character: A Guide to Teaching Your Child Moral Values through Stories*. New York: Touchstone.

Mather, A. and Weldon, L. (2006) *Character Building Day by Day: 180 Quick Read-Alouds for Elementary School and Home*. Minneapolis, MN: Free Spirit.

Prendiville, F. (2000) *Drama and Traditional Story for the Early Years*. London: RoutledgeFalmer.

Schwartz, L. (1990) *What would you Do? A Kid's Guide to Tricky and Sticky Situations*. Huntington Beach, CA: The Learning Works.

Reflective questions

1. How can you use storytelling in your class to promote emotional intelligence?

2. Can you think of stories that you can use to promote empathy? Can you encourage the children to see others' points of view?

3. Are there children in your class that could benefit from bibliotherapy? How will you support them?

4. Can you enlist the help of your librarian or others in your quest to find suitable materials for each of your children's unique needs?

9 Powerful Poetry

Creativity is most necessary in times of emotional hardship, such as when we're frustrated or angry.

Joshua Freedman, 6seconds.org

Poetry is a deal of joy and pain and wonder, with a dash of the dictionary.

Kahlil Gibran

Out of the quarrel with others we make rhetoric; out of the quarrel with ourselves we make poetry.

W. B. Yeats

A poem begins with a lump in the throat.

Robert Frost

Jason's poem

Jason sat down at the table, clearly angry at the world. 'Today we are going to write poetry about the beauty of the world' exclaimed Ms Winston. 'First, we need to brainstorm ...' Jason's mind trailed off. 'Beauty ... what beauty!' he thought ... 'I hate everything and everybody ... the world sucks!' ' Jason,' called Ms Winston, 'I asked you a question.' Jason was suddenly pulled back to reality. 'What?' he whispered. 'Oh yeah, beauty ... um ... nothing comes to mind', he said. 'I don't see anything beautiful. I see only ugliness'. Ms Winston was taken aback but decided to go forward and explore Jason's feelings. 'Well, describe to us the ugliness then.' Jason smirked and complained, 'It is black and cold. It is mean and horrible.' 'OK, now let's see if you can make a poem from that', said Ms Winston.

The Ugly World We Live In by Jason Hall

It is black and cold
It is mean and old
It is lonely and dark
I am a lone lark

Ms Winston was prompted to discuss the poem with Jason. It emerged that Jason's neighbour and best friend had moved to the other side of the country, and Jason was feeling upset. Ms Winston was then able to provide Jason with support through bibliotherapy, journal writing and artistic expressions to help him deal with the strong emotions he was experiencing. What could have led to a downward spiral became a positive sharing event between Ms Winston and Jason.

Poetry as a tool in EQ

Children often express themselves more thoughtfully when writing poetry. A variety of techniques including using two-voice poetry to promote empathy and as a means to reinforce and deepen emotional literacy will be introduced in this chapter, but first let us look at the reason why poetry is a useful tool.

Using poetry to develop and express emotions has a long history in the expressive arts community. Poem therapy is a type of therapy that helps patients express and improve their emotional well-being by reading, writing and analysing poetry (NAPT, 1997). The benefits of poem therapy can be adapted to help children in schools to develop their emotional intelligence.

Reading poems written by others offers a way for children to make connections and associations with the author's work. It allows them to connect with their emotions and understand they are not the only ones who are feeling such emotions. In their own poetry, children may discover channels for troubling thoughts or situations in a non-threatening way. Speaking frankly about emotional situations can be very challenging for some children but poetry gives them an outlet to do so. As Coetzee and Jansen (2007: 89) state, 'A high nurturance classroom environment fosters an open mind and heart. It empowers learners on their journey of self-understanding and self-appreciation. It is an environment where they can share ideas without being judged.'

Poetry to develop empathy

Using poetry to develop empathy is also a wonderful tool for teachers. Ingram (2003:14) states: 'An approach I have found helpful is the introduction of poetry; specifically sociocultural poetry; into the curriculum as a way to reach empathy skills that foster self-understanding and self-acceptance and aid in the process of understanding culturally diverse lived experiences.'

Empathy is a skill all the children in our classes need to learn. Assisting our children to grow into empathetic, compassionate adults is a gift that will help them throughout their lives.

Putting it into practice

Poetry is another form of self-expression. There are many opportunities to use poetry in the classroom to improve emotional intelligence. Bringing emotional intelligence into poetry comes naturally and can really give you insight into your students' feelings and struggles and triumphs! Each child's unique voice will be heard when you introduce these activities.

Promoting emotional literacy through poetry

1. Discuss with children a variety of emotions and what they mean to each person. Perhaps have cards with different emotions written on then.
2. Read children the poem below as an example of a poem based on the word 'mad'.
3. Discuss the similes in the poem.
4. Have children write their own poem based on this poem using an emotion they choose.
5. Display the children's work.

> I'm mad
> I'm mad . . .
> Mad as a swarming beehive
> Mad as the rain belting down from the sky
> Mad as a red streak on a van Gogh
> Mad as a steaming kettle . . . Ready to boil
> I'm mad

Two-voice poems

Two-voice poems are a wonderful way for children to learn about empathy.

1. Share the following poem with the children in your class.
2. Discuss how people can see the same event from completely different points of view.
3. Ask children to work in pairs each taking one point of view of a situation.
4. Together the children can write a two-voice poem.
5. Ask each pair to read the poem aloud in two voices.
6. Discuss the different points of view the poems offer.

> *Jimmy doesn't want to play with me vs. Hey where is Jimmy?*
> Why doesn't he want to play with me?
> > Hey, I wonder where Jimmy is.
> He has so many friends – maybe he forgot about me.
> > I guess he went to play football with the others
> Now I have to spend recess all alone
> > It's much more fun to play together

> *Nervous vs. Well prepared*
> I'm so scared
> > She looks very prepared
> I don't think I can do this
> > I know she will do a great job
> I hope I don't pass out
> > I can see her confidence is growing each day
> OK here it goes
> > What a beautiful presentation
> I did it! Yeah it wasn't so bad
> > She is a natural speaker!

Shape poems

1. Ask children to choose a shape such as a teardrop, heart or lightning bolt that represents an emotion to them.
2. Children write a poem inside or around the edges of the shape that reflect their feelings.

Acrostic poems

1. Brainstorm different emotions with the children.

2. Ask children to write words or phrases that exemplify that emotion beginning with each of the letters of the emotion.

3. Children write and illustrate their poems.

4. Display their work on a Feelings Board.

> *Greedy*
> **G**ive me everything
> **R**ightfully mine
> **E**verything is for me
> **E**veryone else deserves nothing
> **D**ie trying to get more and more and more
> **Y**ou – don't get in my way I need more!

> *Love*
> **L**ots of friends and family
> **O**ur hearts are full of joy
> **V**ery good relationships
> **E**veryone respects each other

EQ theory link

Poetry links into two dimensions of the EQ theory. The in-depth exploration of feelings that takes place during poetry-writing develops self-awareness. By linking feelings with words and images, children can explore deeper meanings in their life experiences. Relationship awareness develops with the use of two-voice poems to explore empathy.

Teacher reflection

I love using poetry in my class. Poems help me to learn about my students' hidden feelings and struggles. Many times, I have been pleasantly surprised that a normally closed student has opened up in a poetry session.

Year 7 teacher

Figure 5: Being Angry – A child's acrostic poem using the word angry.

Recommended reading

Andrews, M. (1996) *Paint a Poem: Imaginative Ideas for the Writing and Presentation of Poetry with Children from Five to Eleven Years*. London: Belair.

Holbrook, S. (2003) *By Definition: Poems of Feelings*. Honesdale, PA: Boyds Mills Press.

Kock, K. and Padgett, R. (1970) *Wishes, Lies and Dreams: Teaching Children to Write Poetry*. New York: Hunter House.

Mecury, F. (2005) *Feelings: A First Poem Book about Feelings*. London: Mecury Books.

Mitton, T. (2005) *I Want to Shout and Stamp about!: Poems About Being Angry (Poemotions)*. London: Hodder Children's Books.

Reflective questions

1. Poetry is an expressive art. How can you incorporate this type of writing into your class?

2. Are there particular children in your class who may open up especially well in this medium? Can you give these children more opportunities to use poetry?

3. Can you change the poetry units you teach so that you explore emotional intelligence skills as well as language skills?

4. How can you effectively display and value your children's poetry?

10 EQ through Songs and Music

He who sings scares away his woes.

Cervantes

Music is what feelings sound like.

Unknown

Music is a higher revelation than all wisdom and philosophy. Music is the electric soil in which the spirit lives, thinks and invents.

Beethoven

Paolo's musical creation

Paolo was angry. His friend Giorgio had just made fun of him in front of all the other boys in his class. He had trusted Giorgio but now he felt betrayed. Paolo felt his stomach tightening ... they had been using instruments to make the sounds of emotions this week and Paolo knew that he could make the sound of his anger very clear by booming it out on the bass and the drums. Paolo ran to the drums and started to bang them with a strong beat. Ms Knowles asked Paolo what the matter was. Paolo replied 'Nothing'. Ms Knowles explained they were going to write songs and put them to music. Paolo decided to write a rap song. Ms Knowles asked them to think of a situation in which the children had felt a strong emotional feeling like love, happiness, jealousy or anger. As Paolo worked on his rap song he felt a release of the tension in his body. Later he stood in front of the class and presented his song that was clearly about the anger he felt and the betrayal of trust. After, Giorgio came to Paolo and apologized. 'I didn't know I would make you so angry', he said. 'It was just a joke.' Paolo felt better, his anger was pushed out of his mind in a positive way.

Music and self-expression

Throughout the ages, music has had a strong connection to emotions. People regularly turn to music to uplift them in happy times or to comfort themselves when sadness strikes. Music affects us all. Recently, scientists have sought to explain the way music influences us at an emotional level. Research that links melody and the mind indicates that listening to and playing music can alter how our brains function. The healing power of music, over body and spirit, is only just beginning to be appreciated. Music therapists have long advocated music to help reduce anxiety and stress as music helps with changing of moods and emotional states to ones that are more positive.

Music permits children to convey emotions that may not be definable through words (Kerr, Walsh and Marshall, 2001). In fact, research on music and emotions proposes that music helps in producing a more relaxed mood and reduces stress (Hanser, 1985). Creating and performing music promotes self-expression and gives pleasure to others. What better way for children to express their feelings in a positive manner than by creating music and songs or listening to music themselves.

Pouliot (1998:146) says that research studies 'do advance the concept that music has the capacity to make us smarter, happier and healthier. Whether it's in terms of enhancing our immune system, reducing our feeling of pain, or heightening our ability to reason and perform logical operations, music may be just the panacea we're all looking for.'

Song lyrics are also important ways to convey messages to children. They enjoy the beat and find it easy to learn the lyrics. 'For me, all music conveys emotion and meaning, even the very easiest pieces. Elementary pieces should contain emotion and meaning both for the listener and for the performer. Perhaps, it could be helpful for a performer to imagine himself outside of his body, as being the listener, and then describe what the listener should feel when he hears this piece played' (Magrath, 2007: 80).

Putting it into practice

Songs and music can help children in many ways. Think about yourself, what do you listen to when you are happy? How about if you are sad or heartbroken? Music is definitely about feelings! Children can use music to develop their emotional intelligence in several ways.

Listening to music/songs

1. Play a variety of short pieces of different types of music.
2. Discuss what emotions each piece makes the children feel.
3. Ask children to bring in a piece of music to class that makes them feel happy. Play parts of each song and discuss with the children how and why each piece feels happy ... is it because of memories, the beat, or the lyrics? Does it inspire dreams or open possibilities?
4. Another day, choose the emotions of sadness, anger, or jealousy and ask children to bring in music to reflect these feelings.
5. Further work can be done by encouraging children to draw or paint while the music is playing.

Musical feelings

1. Play a variety of short musical clips.
2. Pass around a box with various paintings or coloured papers inside. Children can choose either a painting or colours that reflect the music feelings and mood.
3. Children hold up their colour or painting after the music stops and discuss the reasons why the music evokes such feelings. Alternatively, after each piece of music hold a discussion about what type of feelings the music expressed.

Emotional intelligence songs

Another way to use music in the classroom is to introduce EQ songs. Children can also write their own based on a familiar tune. Here are a few written by Helen Maffini:

> *Feelings*
> Happy Feelings
> Happy Feelings
> Make me glad, Make me glad
> See my smiling face, See my smiling face
> Laugh, Laugh, Laugh
> Laugh, Laugh, Laugh
> Sad Feelings, Sad Feelings
> Make me cry, Make me cry
> See my tears streaming, See my tears streaming
> Sigh, Sigh Sigh
> Sigh, Sigh Sigh
> Angry feelings, Angry Feelings
> Make me mad, Make me mad
> See my frowning face,

See my frowning face,
I feel bad,
I feel bad,

I'm Special
I'm a special person can't you see
I am wonderful, there's only one me!
I have hobbies and things I like to do,
Yes, there's only one me and that is true!
And if you get to know me you will see,
Just how wonderful I can be

Making songs

1. Listen to a variety of songs such as rap songs, nursery rhymes or another genre of music.

2. In groups of 3 to 4 children, ask each group to choose an emotion to focus on.

3. Write the lyrics to a song based on the emotion. One way to encourage children is to write the emotion in the form of a story.

4. Put the lyrics to music and perform for the class. Rap is often a good choice for these activities, as are nursery rhymes for the younger children

Making music

1. Children choose from a variety of musical instruments such as tambourines, recorders, drums, bells, triangles, etc.

2. Have a bag filled with emotional literacy words.

3. Children choose a word, and then try to make the sound of that emotion using the instruments. (For example, anger may be drums beating loudly and quickly with all instruments shaking loudly, sadness may be the triangle tinkling softly in the backgrounds of slow drum beat.)

4. Remember there are no right or wrong answers in this activity. Follow each with discussion.

EQ link

Music can help with self-awareness and self-management. By giving children options to express themselves and ways to manage their emotions through music, they will develop these skills and be able to use them independently outside school. You can use music to promote empathy by allowing children to realize that others experience the same feelings as they do and they are not alone.

Teacher reflection

Music is a key component in my teaching. I always play soft music in the background as a soothing and calming technique. I often try to encourage students to present work musically as I find they can express their emotions loud and clear when using this tool!

Year 1 teacher

Recommended reading

Glover, J. and Ward, S. (1998) *Teaching Music in the Primary School* (2nd edn). London: Continuum.

Jensen, E. (2000) *Music with the Brain in Mind*. Thousand Oaks, CA: Corwin Press.

Juslin, P. and Sloboda, J. (2001) *Music and Emotion: Theory and Research*. London: Oxford University Press.

Reflective questions

1. Do you provide opportunities for self-expression through music in your classroom?

2. How can you promote the emotional expression of the children using music or songs?

3. Can you think of any particular children who may benefit from the use of music in order to learn more about their emotions?

4. Why might children enjoy having music as part of their class?

11 EQ through Drama

Acting deals with very delicate emotions. It is not putting up a mask. Each time an actor acts he does not hide; he exposes himself

Rodney Dangerfield

I regard the theatre as the greatest of all art forms, the most immediate way in which a human being can share with another the sense of what it is to be a human being.

Oscar Wilde

To give vent now and then to his feelings, whether of pleasure or discontent, is a great ease to a man's heart.

Francesco Guicciardini

Two emotional outbursts in Ms Lever's classroom

Giovanni's spontaneous play

Giovanni and Luca were playing in the home corner of their classroom. Suddenly Giovanni started shouting 'You can't do anything right! You stupid fool! I'm leaving, I can't take it any more!' With that, he took his hat off the hook and stomped out of the play area. His teacher, Ms Lever, knew that Giovanni's parents were in the midst of a break-up and could see Giovanni's need to express that confusion and anger through his spontaneous role-play. After her careful observations of Giovanni's play episodes, Ms Lever encouraged Giovanni to paint his feelings. Later she shared a story with him that helped him understand that grown-ups have issues and it is not the child's fault in any way. After time, with careful guidance and care Ms Lever saw that Giovanni's play was beginning to return to happier and calmer themes.

Michael faces his bullying problem

Ms Lever often arranged activities for her students to explore issues that arose in the classroom and playground. Recently, Michael was seen bullying several children in different places in the school over a period of a few weeks. Although each issue was dealt with at the time of the incident, Michael didn't seem to be changing his behaviour effectively. Ms Lever called a class meeting and started a discussion about bullying. Without pinpointing any names, she talked about the effects of bullying on both the child who is doing the bullying and those being bullied. She suggested they role-play a bullying situation so they could brainstorm ideas of how to stop it. She purposely chose Michael to play the role of the victim without making it obvious why she had chosen him. During the role-play, Michael seemed shocked when the children started pushing him and calling him names. It seemed that he suddenly realized what effect he was having on the other children. Michael was able at that point to come up with several suggestions to stop bullying, and his behaviour improved in following weeks.

Using drama as a tool to develop EQ

Activities like role-play, scripted drama, presentations and puppet shows are excellent ways to build children's emotional intelligence as they allow children to express their feelings and promote empathy. It is often easier for children to express themselves freely under the guise of another character, a puppet or by pretending to be someone else than to express themselves. This is particularly true of older children who may feel it is easier to say certain things through drama than face-to-face.

As early childhood educators witness, many feelings such as anxiety or stress come out when children play in home corners or other centres in a classroom. However, older children may not have as many opportunities to express such emotions unless we specially cater for them. With teachers' busy timetables, drama is one activity that is easy to build into literacy and language classes, music class or circle times.

Goleman (1995: 36) asserts that 'people who are emotionally adept – who know and manage their own feelings well, and who read and deal effectively with other people's feelings – are at an advantage in any domain of life ... People with well-developed emotional skills are also more likely to be content and effective in their lives, mastering the habits of mind that foster their own productivity; people who cannot marshal some control over their emotional life fight inner battles that sabotage their ability for focused work and clear thought.'

Where drama links to the development of emotional intelligence is in its ability to persuade children to look at events from a number of diverse emotional perspectives. Drama is a tool that can help children to learn about their own emotions, their triggers and reactions. It is also a wonderful tool for developing empathy, as children are encouraged literally to 'step into' someone else's shoes. This promotes the growth of a variety of empathetic skills essential for the development of emotional intelligence.

Drama provides many opportunities to use real situations that further develop children's personal connections. The connections then increase meaning and understanding of the daily events in children's lives in a deeper way. The example of bullying in the story above is one such use.

Putting it into practice

Acting out different scenarios

1. Ask children to choose from a list of scenarios or prepare strips of paper with scenarios for children to choose. For younger children you can use a picture to start discussion.
2. In small groups, ask children to plan a skit to show the scenario. In more advanced groups they can act out from two different perspectives.
3. Children act out the scenarios in front of the class and discussion follows.

Here are some examples you can use:

Imagine you are in the playground. A bully approaches you and demands you give him your snack money. What would you do?

You have a lot of homework this week. You forgot to start working on a big project and you can feel yourself getting anxious.

Your best friend Michelle moved to another school. Now you have no friends at school. You are all alone at recess. You feel lonely and sad. What can you do?

Figure 6: Two children acting out a bullying situation

Emotion charades

1. Provide a variety of emotions on laminated strips of coloured paper in a jar or container.
2. Ask children to form groups of four or five.
3. Children chose an emotion from the container.
4. The children work as a group to develop a skit that displays the emotion.
5. The children act out the skit and the other children try to guess what emotion they were portraying and why.
6. Follow up with discussions about the emotions and why different people feel different emotions surrounding the same event.

Puppet-making

Children can make puppets from socks, wooden spoons, felt and many other materials. They can draw feelings faces on the puppets to encourage discussion of such emotions or they may simply represent different characters.

1. Provide children with a variety of materials to make puppets with or provide ready-made puppets. There are a large range on emotional faced puppets available on the market these days.

2. Encourage children to use their puppets to act out scenarios from stories, problems that have arisen in the classroom and problems they face at home.

3. Allow children time to develop their shows and to perform for others.

Developing playscripts

Part of emotional intelligence is being able to make appropriate decisions and to relate the consequences of your actions. This activity allows children to explore options together as a group in a safe environment and to discuss with others what might be the best option.

1. Develop an open-ended scenario for playwriting in which the characters' decision can be written from multiple perspectives (for example, a child witnesses a group of boys teasing another boy, he can choose to join in, go to tell a teacher, help the boy himself, etc.).

2. Ask children to write at least three different endings to the same scenario.

3. Let the children act out the scenarios to the class and discuss the different options. Ask children to decide on the best option in each case.

EQ theory link

Drama develops self-awareness and relationship-awareness in children by allowing them to recognize their feelings and discover inner emotions while acting out various scenes. Relationship awareness also comes into play as children role-play situations, as they may not have thought of how their actions affect others. They can also learn to be more empathetic by seeing things from another point of view. Finally, children can learn decision-making skills through drama.

Teacher reflection

I have found that drama is a key tool in letting children express their feelings. Students who would normally feel too timid to express their opinions find taking on the role of another person allows for full expression of the emotions they have had bottled up inside.

Drama teacher

Recommended reading

Bany-Winters, L. (1997) *On Stage: Theatre Games and Activities for Kids*. Chicago, IL: Chicago Review Press.

Rooyackers, H. and Bowman, C. (1997) *101 Drama Games for Children: Fun and Learning with Acting and Make-Believe*. New York: Hunter House.

Salas, Jo (1999) *Improvising Real Life: personal Story in Playback Theatre* (3rd edn). New Paltz, NY: Tusitala.

Reflective questions

1. If you work with young children, do they have ample opportunity to role-play? Do you take time out to observe children's spontaneous acting?

2. Do you provide the time and resources necessary for your students to express their emotions in a non-threatening manner?

3. How could you incorporate drama into your emotional literacy programme?

4. Are there situations in your class in which acting may help to promote empathy?

12 EQ through Art

The artist is a receptacle for the emotions that come from all over the place: from the sky, from the earth, from a scrap of paper, from a passing shape, from a spider's web.

Pablo Picasso

Art is one of the sources through which the soul expresses itself and inspires others. But to express art thoroughly, one must have the inner emotions opened thoroughly.

Meher Baba

Painting is just another way of keeping a diary.

Pablo Picasso

Every artist dips his brush in his own soul, and paints his own nature into his pictures.

Henry Ward Beecher

Maggie's painting

Maggie was having a bad day. In the morning, her mother had yelled at her because she was too tired to get out of bed for school. She had felt anger boiling up in her stomach as she hurried to get ready before the bus came. At school, she realized she had forgotten her homework on her bedside table. Her chest tightened and she felt tears well up in her eyes. 'Again?' complained Ms Jones with distaste in her voice. 'Maggie you are a very forgetful young lady!' The words stung Maggie's heart. 'Why am I so stupid?' she thought. 'I can't do anything right.' Maggie couldn't think straight for the rest of the morning. Ms Jones's words kept replaying in her mind.

At least it was art today. Maggie always enjoyed Mrs Stammer's class. Today the children looked at pictures by Monet. Maggie felt calm as she admired the soft pastel colours and imagined herself in the gardens. Mrs Stammers encouraged the children to think about a time when they had strong feelings and what colours they felt at the time. All the emotions of the day came rushing back. It was Maggie's turn to paint. Maggie took the red paint and splashed it on the paper angrily. All her emotions spilled on to the page. Maggie drew a volcano with herself emerging from the top-large splotches of red fire everywhere. Mrs Stammers was shocked at the emotion on the paper. After class, she asked Maggie to stay behind. Mrs Stammers talked with Maggie about where the ideas from her picture had come from. She explained how all her frustration of the day had made her feel she was going to explode and it had all come out in the painting. Mrs Stammers took special care to talk with Maggie about her feelings and encouraged her to make a portfolio of paintings that reflected her feelings. She was also able to show Ms Jones her painting and explain where some of her frustration came from. Ms Jones was shocked. Had she really spoken that way to a child? She knew Maggie was forgetful but she didn't realize the impact her words were having on the children in her class.

Art and emotions

Throughout history, both children and adults have used art as a way of expressing their deepest emotions. The majority of people feel the need to express themselves, not just for enjoyment, but also to identify and deal with pain. Art therapy is an effective strategy to cope with stress, emotional trauma, helplessness and other anxieties. Let's think about ways we can witness art helping children in a classroom:

- A young boy paints tear drops on a plaster mask after he recently lost his beloved pet dog.
- A kindergarten student draws a happy face on her wooden spoon puppet after sharing her toy with a new girl in the class.
- A six-year-old girl draws a picture of her mother with a large black marker indicating a tumour diagnosed recently.
- An eight-year-old boy makes a collage with pictures of rainbows, blue skies and gold medals and words such as success and happiness written with cut-out magazine letters after winning the race on sports day.
- A 13-year-old girl builds a display box with pictures and keepsakes of her sister to cope with her death a few months ago in a car accident.

Riley (1999) constructs a powerful line of reasoning for employing the creative arts as a teaching tool for children of all ages. Riley shows that an essential characteristic in selecting teaching strategies is to utilize techniques that children will 'accept'. The arts supply an integrated feeling of curiosity, enjoyment and hands-on participation from which children benefit. Children contribute and construct a product.

There are numerous benefits achieved by using art to help children deal with stressful situations.

1. Children develop a sense of personal achievement: Generating a real product that expresses feelings can develop confidence and cultivate feelings of self-worth. Children experience self-fulfilment from the artistic process of being creative and analysing reasons behind the product they have created.

2. It offers a sense of self-control and reflection: Art can help children visually articulate emotions and fears that they cannot express through traditional methods. By using the medium of art children can gain a feeling of control over the situations they are facing. They can also reflect on their artwork and perhaps realize the extent of their emotions and the triggers for such feelings.

3. Art can reduce the intensity or amount of stressful feelings: Frequent stress can be detrimental to both our psyche and our body. Insomnia, anxiety, depression and weakened immune systems are all possible results from living in a state of high stress. However, we also have learned that artistic pursuits can augment amounts of serotonin in the brain. Any activity that increases serotonin is likely to be beneficial, as it fights depression.

Putting it into practice

Many children express themselves in non-verbal ways and we as teachers need to provide outlets for expressing emotions through these other outlets. Art is one manner of expression in which many children feel comfortable. The specific strategies we suggest below are ways that you can use to release trapped emotions, or turn them into something we can better understand. Art is a form of emotional expression. Emotional expression is a part of developing emotional intelligence.

Clay modelling

Working with clay is therapeutic and relaxing. Children can express themselves in any manner by using this type of medium. The actual use of clay reduces stress and anxiety in both adults and children. As a teacher, using clay in your classroom provides another outlet for tension and stress to fade away.

1. Play relaxing music in the background.

2. Give each child a ball of clay.

3. Ask children to massage the clay while thinking about a strong feeling they have experienced recently.

4. Children can create any representation of the feeling they experienced with their clay ball.

5. After clay has dried, ask children to paint their artwork. The colours used will also help to express the emotion more clearly.

6. Any child who wishes to share his or her feelings with the class should be encouraged to do so.

Painting/drawing and emotional literacy

Allowing children to paint and draw to express happenings in their lives is a valuable tool. Children can express feelings of being torn apart by divorce, low self-esteem, being bullied and many other things through pictures instead of words. They say a picture says as much as 1,000 words, and this is certainly true if children are

Figure 7: A girl draws a picture of feeling torn apart by her parents' divorce

Figure 8: A kindergarten student feels upset at leaving his parents at the start of school

expressing themselves fully. The pictures above express a child's feeling of being torn between her parents going through a divorce, and another child's feeling of helplessness starting school and being separated from his family. The emotions these pictures express show us the depth of expression that children can portray through artistic endeavours.

1. Discuss with children different emotions. What images can they think of that would represent such emotions (e.g. an erupting volcano or a lightning bolt for anger, rain for sadness, sunshine for happiness)? What could emotions look like?

2. If possible show pictures on an interactive whiteboard or from magazines, and discuss the emotions that are felt and why. Do colours play any part in these feelings? You can also introduce pictures by great artists such as *The Scream* (Munch), *Starry Night* (Van Gogh), *The Dream* (Picasso) and many others. You can discuss the emotions portrayed.

3. Give children as many opportunities as possible to draw or paint their own feelings and express themselves artistically as well as verbally or in writing.

Artistic reflection on literature

You can use art as a response to stories and happenings in the classroom as well. After reading stories in the classroom discuss the emotions certain characters may have felt.

1. Ask the children to imagine how characters in the story may have felt. Discuss in small groups and then bring the discussion to the whole class.

2. Give children the opportunity to produce a collage, paint or draw how they perceive the character may have felt.

3. You can use this to express situations that happen at school (e.g. bullying, fights, feeling left out, etc.) and can help children to become more empathetic of others.

EQ theory Link

By using artistic mediums to express themselves children become more self-aware. Realizing the impact different colours have on mood and using art as a means of managing emotions is an excellent tool for children to use. What better way to express anger without hurting one's self or others than through painting or clay works?

Teacher reflection

We all have problems; however most children, especially boys, do not want to admit this or to share their feelings. I have found that eventually, with frequent use and guidance from a teacher, art can really help most children to express themselves and to allow a release of their emotions in ways they may not have been able to do verbally or by writing.

Primary art teacher

Recommended reading

Carroll, C. (2001) *How Artists See Feelings: Joy Sadness Fear Love*. New York: Abbeville Kids.

Heegaard, M. (2003) *Drawing Together to Learn About Feelings*. Minneapolis, MN: Fairview Press.

McNiff, S. (2004) *Art Heals: How Creativity Cures the Soul*. Boston, MA: Shambhala.

Sunderland, M. (1997) *Draw on Your Emotions*. Brackley: Speechmark.

Reflective questions

1. How can you bring artistic expression into your daily lessons?

2. Are there activities that you could give children a choice in how they express themselves?

3. What can you do to encourage the children to express themselves more artistically?

4. Do you encourage all types of learners to express their emotions?

13 Projects that Matter

The only reason we are so different is because of different experiences. They create the software of our souls.

Deepak Chopra

The art of teaching is the art of assisting discovery

Mark Van Doren

The important thing is to not stop questioning

Albert Einstein

The cold hospital ward

Tim was an active boy in Mrs James's class. He was in Year 5 and had a very good relationship with most of the children in his class. After some time Mrs James realized that he was not himself. He was tired, pale, bad-tempered and was going to the bathroom more often. Mrs James was very concerned and since Tim came from a single-parent home, she called his mother to inform her of her observations. Tim didn't come to school next day. When Mrs James called home to ask about him, his mother sounded very upset, Tim had been diagnosed with diabetes and had been admitted to hospital with a high blood-sugar level.

Mrs James went to visit him in hospital next day, taking with her a small jigsaw puzzle, as she knew that Tim enjoyed solving puzzles in class. As she was leaving, she paid close attention to the appearance of the ward. She noticed that it wasn't really child-friendly. It looked dull with boring, beige-coloured walls with no posters or drawings. She passed by what was called a playroom and there were no toys or games around, no books, not even beanbags or a rug to provide a warm ambience. It was a bare, cold room with a couple of sofas and a TV screen hanging from the ceiling. She felt sorry for the sick children who were sitting there looking bored; the TV was not showing a cartoon or other age-appropriate programme.

Next day, Mrs James talked to the class about Tim's medical condition. She also talked to them about what she had seen and how she felt while she was in the children's ward.

The class was silent for a few seconds. Then one of the children asked, 'But what's diabetes? How do you get diabetes?' Another child asked in a sad voice whether Tim could be cured. A third child asked 'When will Tim come back to school?'

Mrs James listened to all their questions; she assured them that Tim would be back at school once he felt better. She saw that this was an opportunity to teach the children a set of skills. They could learn about the ability to empathize and give, to improve communication and teamwork skills, as well as do a meaningful project through which academic skills could be developed.

She discussed the whole issue with the children and listened carefully to their suggestions. In the end, the class agreed to do some research on diabetes and share their findings with each other through presentations. They also decided to do some fund-raising activities so that they could all contribute to creating a more child-friendly atmosphere in the children's ward. The children got excited when they found out that they would be able to go with Mrs James to visit Tim in hospital and that she would take them to see the empty playroom. The rest of the lesson was used to prepare *Get Well Soon* cards for Tim.

Four days later Tim rejoined the class. He was welcomed in a very special way and was soon engrossed in all the different fundraising activities the class was planning.

Three weeks later the children, working in groups, put on show. The show included a presentation on diabetes, a song written and composed by the children with Mrs James's help, and a sketch written by one of the groups and acted out by the whole class. The audience, comprising parents, children from other classes and year groups and teachers, was greatly moved. Funds were raised through the sale of tickets to the event.

At the end of the show, it was announced that the class had set up a toy corner and that donations for this were invited. Children were asked to produce happy, lively paintings that could be framed and hung on the walls of the ward, to show that there were children outside who cared.

 This whole project took a month to complete. It was a lot of hard work, but it was well worthwhile. As Tim commented 'even though I was sick, I got to know how much Mrs James and my class cared for me'.

Developing children's emotional intelligence will not take place if children spend all their time in the classroom with the teacher, following a course book. Children need to have the opportunity to practise their emotional and social skills in real-life situations where they can be challenged yet guided to enhance their EQ skills. Since it is the teacher's responsibility to orchestrate the whole learning experience, they also need to be supported by a school system and administration that appreciates such efforts and makes such tasks possible.

Planning real-life experiences for the children requires teachers to have some background knowledge about the children, areas of strength and the areas they need to develop, their talents and interests, their culture, the different needs of the community, project opportunities, any restrictions or regulations, etc. Moreover, teachers need to take into account a number of prerequisites that can contribute to the success or failure of the whole learning process.

Most importantly, you need to have a clear vision about what contributes to developing children's EQ, what are the EQ components and the different strategies and tools you can use to enhance children's EQ, and how to record and monitor children's progress. When these concepts are clear, you can make a clear list of the emotional and social skills appropriate to the age group you teach and plan to enhance them through real-life learning projects. A lot has been written on this, starting from Goleman's book *Emotional Intelligence* (1995) to so many others mentioned in our suggested reading list and the references at the back of this book.

Creating real-life learning opportunities

To create real-life experiences for children, you need to keep an eye out for every classroom opportunity that can be used to develop a real-life project like the one mentioned in the story above. Here are some factors that can contribute into the success of real-life projects:

1. Children's safety and security must be kept as top priority at all times.

2. The emotional social skills to be developed through the project must be clearly specified, preferably for each individual child.

3. An environment of trust must to be created, where all those involved are respected and appreciated.

4. The project must be relevant to children's life, their enthusiasm and interest.

5. The learning experience must be meaningful and have real-life value to the children and perhaps to whoever is involved in the project

6. The outcome of the project should make sense to those involved, and will ideally have some positive benefit for others. These projects may be hands-on work in the community, where children can see and feel the beneficial effect of their work on the community.

7. All efforts should be recognized and appreciated.

In addition to real-life projects that can take children beyond the school's walls, you can also use real-life situations that occur between the children to develop their EQ. Different incidents can take place in the classroom, in the corridors, during break time, during field trips, during after-school activities, just to name a few. These all can be precious opportunities to allow genuine learning to take place. Examples of these incidents can be: an argument or a fight between two children, losing someone precious or a pet, being a bully, being bullied, having someone seriously sick in the family, going through divorce, low self-esteem, etc. These are all examples of real-life situations that children go through every day, and in many cases they find themselves helpless or very confused, and in desperate need of a teacher's support and guidance. Children learn from these situations much more than from artificial activities simply because they are all real. The learning experience is meaningful to them and it affects their life and their relationships with others in school.

Putting it into practice

Giving a helping hand

1. Divide the children into groups.
2. Each group will study an opportunity of giving a helping hand. This can be helping at an old people's home, an orphanage, or helping people affected by a natural disaster like a flood, earthquake, tsunami, etc.
3. Each group will study the size of the problem, its causes, and what they can do to help.
4. Each group will then prepare a written report/article on their findings and interpretations.
5. Each group presents their findings and their plan of help to the rest of the class.
6. The teacher guides and helps all groups to execute their plans, making sure that children are always kept safe and secure.
7. Their work can be published in local newspapers, a school journal, a yearbook or even a class journal.

My dream job

1. Brainstorm with the children the kinds of jobs that they know. Videos relating to different jobs can be used to develop awareness.
2. Help the children to think of the kind of job they want to have when they grow up.

3. Try to arrange for children to visit a variety of workplaces in accordance with their job preferences, to enable them to get a feeling for the working environment and to talk to people who are working there. Parents can be involved in these visits.

4. If visits are not possible, invite people doing different jobs to visit your class. Make sure that the children get to ask the questions they want. Some of these speakers can be parents of some of the children in your class. Hotseating, where the child then pretends to be the person and answers questions is also very helpful.

5. The children then can draw pictures of themselves in their ideal workplace or they can role-play their dream jobs in groups.

6. They can also dress up in their new job uniform/outfit and talk to the class about their real future plans, mentioning the kinds of skills, knowledge and qualifications they will need to have to be able to make their dreams come true.

Friendship fair

1. Discuss with children the importance of friendships. What qualities should we look for in a friend? How can we be a good friend? Reflect on the true meaning of friendship.

2. Literature can be shared with children relating to friendship. This can be shared in literature circles in the classroom or through written responses.

Figure 9: Items made during a friendship fair

Figure 10: Two children presenting their work on friendship

3. Plan a fair with the class based around the true meaning of friendship.

4. Children can write poetry, find quotes, write about their perceptions on friendship, write songs and prepare display boards.

5. Hold a fair where parents can come to see the children's work or other classes can come to visit.

6. Encourage children to present their work to others.

7. This idea can be used with any other topic you find suitable or the children express an interest in e.g. bullying, kindness, prejudice, helpfulness, etc.

EQ theory link

To carry out real-life projects children need to interact with other children and adults. This will contribute to developing their social and relationship management skills. Some projects like 'Giving a helping hand' teach the children to be empathic and care and support others. 'My dream job' develops children's self-awareness and helps create self-motivation to achieve their goals in life. 'My friendship fair' helps build awareness of relationships with others and how to maintain and manage good relationships.

Teacher reflection

I have incorporated community service learning into my Year 4 class with amazing results. Children are very giving and have increased their organization and thinking skills as well as empathy skills.

Year 4 teacher

Recommended reading

Bourne, B. (2000) *Taking Inquiry Outdoors: Reading, Writing, and Science beyond the Classroom Walls*. Portland, ME: Stenhouse.

Helem, J.H. and Katz, L.G. (2001) *Young Investigators: The Project Approach in the Early Years*. New York: Teachers College Press.

Lambert, N. M. and McCombs, B. L. (1998) *How Students Learn: Reforming Schools through Learner-centered Education*. Washington, DC: American Psychological Association.

Lieberman, G. and Hoody, Linda. (1998) *Closing the Achievement Gap: Using the environment as an integrated Context for Learning*. Poway, CA: Science Wizards.

Littky, D. and Grabelle, S. (2004) *The Big Picture*. Alexandria, VA: Association for Supervision and Curriculum Development.

Reflective questions

1. Do you think it's important to develop children's EQ? If yes, how can you convince someone who believes otherwise?

2. Do you think assigning children to real-life projects is important? If so, please justify?

3. In your context, what kind of real-life projects can you develop with the children you teach? In addition, what kinds of EQ skills are you aiming for? Share your ideas with others in your group.

4. What are the points that you need to be careful of while planning real-life projects?

5. Children's life in school is also part of their real life. Can you think of any projects that are real-life but are still within the school boundaries?

6. What effects can real-life projects have on children's emotional and social development?

14 Home–School Links

Families and teachers might wish that the school could do the job alone. But today's school needs families, and today's families need the school. In many ways, this mutual need may be the greatest hope for change.

Dorothy Rich

The emotional literacy of young people is more likely to grow when their parents can help them negotiate the different messages they receive from school, their family and elsewhere.

The Emotional Literacy Handbook

Parents are a child's first teachers.

Unknown

Brian's story

Brian Fisher's parents were both successful. Brian had a younger brother who was two years old. Both parents were working outside the home, and Ms Goll noticed that Brian did his homework only sporadically. Although Ms Goll required all parents to initial each page of homework, this was rarely done. Ms Goll decided to call Brian's parents for a meeting at the school.

Both parents showed up looking very concerned. It was clear they loved Brian and had his best interests at heart. As Ms Goll began to mention the unfinished homework and unsigned sheets, Brian's parents looked sheepish. 'We didn't realize it was that important, I mean he is only in Year 2' said Mr Fisher. Ms Goll went on to explain the importance of home–school links. She showed the Fishers research showing just how important parents are in their child's education. The Fishers looked embarrassed. 'We had no idea', they said. 'We thought we would let him be totally independent from the very beginning.' Ms Goll knew all too well that even educated, successful parents like the Fishers may not be aware of just how important their roles are.

Ms Goll decided to hold a parents' meeting for all the children in her class. Before the meeting, she prepared a list of activities parents could do at home to support their children. She had volunteer sheets for parents to sign up for different activities. She photocopied several articles that showed recent research on student achievement and how it correlates with parental involvement. She also gave the parents an email address to contact her and encouraged the parents to write to her if they had any queries or questions about how to help their child.

Home–school partnerships and EQ

An ever-mounting quantity of research presents the numerous benefits that take place when parents are involved in their children's schooling. Comer (1984) proposes that when families and teachers collaborate, this creates the emotional support that children need in order to learn effectively. As educators, we need to be aware that children see immense benefits when parents work closely with the schools and this leads to a more emotionally settled child in the classroom (Simich-Dudgeon, 1986).

Hoover-Dempsey and Sandler (1997) explained that some facets are vital in making parent–school partnerships successful. Schools ought to assist parents in realizing that it is their responsibility as parents to become a partner in their child's education. Schools must communicate with parents what they are seeking to accomplish in teaching emotional literacy in order to ensure that parents comprehend the objectives and the processes (Weare, 2004).

Making parents feel welcome

Many parents stay away because they indicate that they do not feel welcome at the school. While schools usually state that parents are welcome, the truth may be entirely different. Schools can do many things to make parents feel welcome, for example:

1. Provide a parental ambassador to synchronize communication involving parents and schools is an effective way to build relationships that can flourish.

2. Create a parents' room or area that would offer coffee or refreshments, parenting books, brochures on children's development or nutrition, for example, and simple volunteer activities that parents could complete while visiting or lists to sign up for other volunteer activities.

3. Create a lending library for parents to borrow resources that could help them promote EQ at home. For example stories, videos, puppets and games especially as they relate to EQ.

4. Organize parent workshops not only to clarify aspects of the curriculum but also general workshops that contribute into better understanding of their roles as parents, and how they can help their children to have a happier and more successful life. Examples include: How to promote EQ at home, Your child's emotional development, and Your child's brain: the latest developments in brain research.

5. Develop activities for parents and children to complete together at home promoting emotional intelligence that are then shared with the children's classmates.

6. Sending home newsletters focusing on emotional intelligence and activities parents can do to support children at home.

7. Encouraging parents to take part at the school in real-life projects that aim at enhancing children's EQ. Parents can also accompany children on field trips related to these projects.

Putting it into practice

Parents are a vital part of their children's lives. They are the first source of a child's moral and character development. Research showing the benefits of home–school partnerships is clear: when parents are highly involved in children's education they receive better results (Weare, 2004). The activities and strategies suggested here invite child/parent collaboration.

Family treasure box

Children and parents can work together to create a family treasure box that can then be brought to school and shared. They can decorate the box with photos, familiar sayings used at home, names and other important places, maps and any other relevant items. Together the family can put in letters to each other, photos, important mementos from trips or fun places they have visited together. Later when the class comes together, the children explain the significance of the items in the box and the process by which they made the box. As a result children learn a great deal of personal information about each other, what is important to them and their family and it gives them a chance to discuss their feelings about certain family members.

Figure 11: Three siblings making their family treasure box

Figure 12: The finished box

A home–school project

Parents and children come together to create a project that is relevant to their community and promotes a joint sense of purpose. Examples such as framing children's artwork to hang in the local hospital, laminating children's pictures to use as placemats, or creating a gift box to present to a needy family can be made together with the help of parents in the class. For improved emotional intelligence, discussion is key, and reflection on why such a project is being undertaken.

Newsletters

Newsletters can be a key communication vehicle for schools to make contact and connections with all parents. Tailor-made newsletters can explore the issues of self-esteem, self-worth, empathy and other emotional intelligence components. Follow-up activities given to parents and children to complete together at home can stress the importance of these attributes. When schools emphasize the importance of EQ in newsletters rather than solely on academics, they show parents what they value.

Family circle time

Schools should encourage discussion to take place about important emotional issues at home as well as at school. One way to do this is by encouraging families to participate in a family circle time, similar to class meetings but held in the home. There are many ways to run a family meeting such as the parent introducing a topic they feel they would like to discuss, or children arranging the agenda themselves. It is useful if teachers and parents communicate regularly about issues arising at school or home so parents and teachers can address the issues effectively in both settings. The important thing to consider is that all parties are respectful and listen carefully to one another. Parents should be encouraged not to make judgements but at times to give children another perspective or guide them to think about consequences of actions that they may not have considered.

EQ theory link

Home–school links promote the relationship awareness and management of the child. By developing a strong awareness of the relationship between school and home, children will benefit in many ways. They can learn how they can benefit from the use of better communication between all parties and how to manage their relationships with family members more effectively.

Parent reflection

On learning about emotional intelligence and its importance to my kids, I decided to implement a weekly circle time with my family. Every Saturday we wrote a topic we wanted to discuss on a strip of paper and placed it in a box we called our Circle Time box. Then we sat together, pulled each slip of paper out of the box, and discussed it. I felt my children gained more confidence and were able to confide in me in ways they hadn't before.

Parent of two primary schoolchildren

Recommended reading

Allen, J. (2007) *Creating Welcoming Schools: A Practical Guide to Home–School Partnerships with Diverse Families*. New York: Teachers College Press.

Childre, D. L. (1995) *A Parenting Manual*. Boulder Creek, CA: Planetary Publications.

Epstein, J., Sanders, M., Simon, B., Salinas, K., Jansorn, N. and Van Voorhis, F. (2002) *School, Family, and Community Partnerships: Your Handbook for Action* (2nd edn). Alexandria, VA: Corwin Press.

Lawrence-Lightfoot, S. (2004) *The Essential Conversation: What Parents and Teachers Can Learn from Each Other?* New York: Ballantine Books.

Swap McAllister, S. (1993) *Developing Home–School Partnerships: From Concepts to Practice*. New York: Teachers College Press.

Reflective questions

1. In what way can parents and educators in your school collaborate to enhance children's emotional intelligence?

2. What kind of concerns (if any) do you think might create an obstacle in creating such partnership?

3. Do you require support from your school administration? How will you go about getting it?

4. What are the expected outcomes of creating home–school partnerships? Think in terms of outcomes, for the children, for the school, for the teachers and for the parents.

5. What differences do you notice between the children whose parents are highly involved and those who do not appear to take part in their child's education? How can you share these observations with others?

15 The Power of Reflection

The real voyage of discovery consists not of seeing new landscapes, but in having new eyes.

Marcel Proust

A defining condition of being human is that we have to understand the meaning of our experience.

Jack Mezirow

Getting a smile back

Mrs Brown is a Year 2 teacher. She has 18 children in her class. She also has an assistant teacher with whom she works very closely throughout the day. The children in her class are of mixed abilities and come from different backgrounds. She has eight different nationalities in her class.

Understanding the children was a top priority for Mrs Brown and her assistant. To this end, they both developed the habit of observing the children closely and recording as much information as possible. They also reflected daily on their practice and on each child's performance to ensure that they could meet all the children's needs.

Part of their everyday routine is to assign 10 to 20 minutes at the end of the day to write their reflections. They then share and discuss their thoughts. One afternoon, while carrying out their end-of-day reflections they realized that Salma hadn't been herself lately. She hadn't been very active. She had also missed doing her homework a couple of times. In fact, she seemed to be rather unhappy.

The next day Salma came to class. Both teachers observed her closely. They realized that she seemed to have problems with some of the girls in her class. Her classmates started to exclude her. One girl was particularly nasty to her when they had to work together. Mrs Brown felt that Salma was deeply hurt and very upset. At this stage, Mrs Brown intervened in support of Salma and was able to resolve the situation.

After class, Mrs Brown spent some time with Salma in an attempt to find out what the problem was. Salma was in tears. At first, she couldn't speak, but then she opened up, telling her teacher how badly some of the girls had treated her. A group of girls, who called her names, hid her lunch box and turned her best friend against her, was bullying her. She spent break times alone. Being all alone, she didn't know what to do and spent most of her time hiding in the bathroom. For Salma, school was becoming a real nightmare.

Mrs Brown was very concerned and promised to help solve the problem. She decided to raise the issue in class meetings, through storytelling and other means but without singling Salma out. Salma's peers started to accept her once again. She started smiling again; Mrs Brown was relieved and delighted.

The story above illustrates a teacher engaging in reflective practice; a very important skill if we are to understand the children we teach. It also illustrates helping children to self-reflect and find answers to their problems. Reflection is one of the primary skills for building children's EQ. Ellison (2001) considers reflection as one of the basic building blocks of social and emotional competence. She states that 'Self-reflective capacities on the one hand and the ability to recognize what others are thinking and feeling on the other provide the foundation for children to understand, manage and express the social and emotional aspects of life.'

What is reflection?

Reflection is a mental process children can go through to look back at an experience and construct their own meaning. After reflecting, they can define what they have learnt from the experience and perhaps see how they can do things differently to improve their learning experience. In *Habits of Mind* (2000: 17), Costa and Kallick state that 'to be reflective means to mentally wander through where you have been and try to make sense out of it'. They also emphasize the role that reflection has in helping children to be producers of meaning rather than consumers of knowledge.

'In teaching reflection skills the role of the teacher becomes a facilitator, who guides the children through the learning experience. The teacher helps each child monitor individual progress, construct meaning from the content learned and from the process of learning it, and apply the learnings to other contexts and settings' Costa and Kallick (2000:16).

The relationship between the teacher and the children has a profound effect on their reflection, as the whole process requires the children to be honest with themselves and with the teacher and to express their thoughts and feelings without any kind of fear or hesitation. Thus, trust, acceptance and not being judgemental are essential qualities that teachers need to have if they are to encourage the children to be reflective.

How can teachers guide children through reflection?

Creating a class environment where children are encouraged to reflect and are welcomed to share their reflections with others can play a vital role in the success of the whole process. In addition, children need to see models of reflective adults around them who can speak their thoughts aloud or write their journals and share their reflections with them. They need to learn that we all learn from the experiences we go through and modify our perceptions and acts.

To guide children through the process of reflection you need to keep an open eye on everyday class opportunities where children go through an experience that can teach them and others. Alternatively, you can create these situations through different activities like the ones suggested below. After the experience, invite the children to step out of the situation and look at it from a distance. They need to think about the experience, what they did, how they felt, what they thought, what they could have done differently and what they learnt from this experience

Here are some examples of questions that children can ask themselves while reflecting:

- How did I feel? How do I feel now?
- Why do I feel the way I do?
- How do I see my acts?
- What does this tell me? What did I learn from this experience?
- If I go through this experience again would I do anything differently?
- If so, what would I do differently and why?

After reflecting, they can express their reflection orally, through drawing or in writing. Younger children, who have not yet developed their writing skills, can express their reflection orally or through drawings. It is also a good idea to encourage the children to talk about their drawings as adults might interpret children's drawings differently. They might not always see what the child is trying to communicate.

Older children who are more confident with their writing abilities can express their reflections through journal writing. Yet, we still have to remember that they all have their own preferred ways of reflection. Once you get to know the children in your class well, you will learn their preferred manner of reflection. Giving the children various opportunities of expressing their reflection can make their task more interesting. These can be in forms of individual task reflection, group discussion, teacher–child discussion, counselling, or children interviewing each other, etc.

Saving reflections and storing them in the children's portfolio so that you can monitor the development of the skill as well as their overall progress is a wonderful idea. It is very rewarding to see how children grow emotionally and socially, and how their reflections lead them to choose their acts rather than being 'reflexive', to use Robert Sylwester's (1997b) term by which he means reacting at the least provocation.

Putting it into practice

Self-interview

Invite each child to sit in front of a mirror, or use small hand mirrors. Children can do this activity in pairs as well.

1. Let each child ask himself some questions such as the ones mentioned above. Print the questions on coloured paper and laminate them, as you may need to use this activity when opportunities arise. For younger children ask them to choose sad, happy or angry faces and think about how they felt and what they looked like when they felt that way in the past.

2. Let the children share their reflections

3. This is a wonderful opportunity for you to get to know more about the children, their thinking skills, their thinking patterns and their self-image.

4. If you notice anything significant, you can record your observation and then use the information to give appropriate help to the child.

Reflection chair

You can use this activity to let the children think about their behaviour when they misbehave or reflect on their achievements. It is very important to use the reflective

Figure 13: A young girl remembers a time she felt angry

chair for both positive and negative performance. Getting the children to use the chair only when they misbehave creates negative connotations with learning how to reflect. Invite the child, after reflection, to share his thoughts and feelings in whatever way you find most appropriate, such as writing his journal, filling in a form, talking to you, or sharing orally with the rest of the children.

I'm a puppet

Some children find it difficult to express themselves directly. One way of helping these children is to use puppets. Let the child give the puppet a name. Ask the child to imagine that he is the puppet going through the same life experience that the child did. Encourage him to reflect and talk about his feelings and thoughts. If you find a child is stuck you can encourage him to talk through the scenario asking questions such as those listed on page 103.

EQ theory link

Reflection activities come under developing self-awareness and self-management components in the framework. Children become more aware of their behaviour, their feelings and patterns of thinking. Once this becomes a mind habit, it will lead to better self-management and improved relationships with others.

Recommended reading

Brandt, R. (1998) *Powerful Learning*. Alexandria, VA: Association for Supervision and Curriculum Development.

Costa, A. L. and Kallick, B. (2000) *Habits of Mind*. Alexandria, VA: Association for Supervision and Curriculum Development.

Damasio, A. (1999) *The Feeling of What Happens*. New York: Harcourt.

de Bono, Edward (1993) *Teach Your Child How To Think*. London: Penguin.

Doty, G. (2001) *Fostering Emotional Intelligence in K-8 Students*. Thousand Oaks, CA: Corwin Press.

Ellison, L. (2001) *The Personal Intelligence*. Thousand Oaks, CA: Corwin Press.

Katta, M. (2000) *Stop! Think! Choose! Building Emotional Intelligence in Young Children*. Tucson, AZ: Zephyr Press.

Reflective questions

1. As a teacher how often do you reflect on your practices?

2. Do you think reflection is a useful strategy for teachers? Why/Why not?

3. Would you teach reflection to the children you teach? Please justify.

4. What strategies would you follow when teaching reflection?

5. How can you share a child's reflection with parents/guardians?

6. How can reflection contribute in developing a child's EQ?

16 The Art of Observation

A mysterious painting

Mrs Neil looked puzzled as she was looking deeply into Leena's artwork. In fact, she was very concerned. She took the painting to her assistant and asked if she knew what the little girl was going through. Unfortunately, she did not know either.

Leena's depiction of herself as a sad little girl with a line cutting her in two would not leave Mrs Neil.

By nature, Leena was a lively girl with a keen sense of humour. Her tendency to giggle, her beautiful smile and her shining eyes had always endeared her to the teacher.

Mrs Neil's first thought was to talk to the girl. Nevertheless, she decided that the child might not be ready for that, so instead she started to observe her. She observed her working with her group. She observed her working individually. She even observed her during recess. Leena did not really seem to be herself. Mrs Neil's anxiety grew upon seeing that Leena had lost all interest in the PE lesson, a lesson that she had previously always enjoyed. During lunchtime, Leena did not seem to have much appetite. It became clear that something was seriously wrong.

That day at break, Mrs Neil asked Leena about her drawing. Leena looked at it and didn't find much to say at first. After a while, she said, 'I really don't know what to do. If I choose to go with Dad, Mum will feel bad. If I stay with my mum, Dad might get sick. You see he loves me too!' Mrs Neil wiped away the little girl's tears. She gave Leena a hug and made her feel that she would always be there for her. She also asked her to write her journal every day, talking about all her thoughts and feelings.

Just before leaving, Leena asked if she could stick the picture she had drawn in her journal and Mrs Neil said, 'Of course you can', with a smile of sorrow at what the girl was going through.

As educators, we need to develop a clear picture about the children in our care. You can use different tools and strategies to achieve this. However, one of the most powerful tools is observation. 'Getting to know the children we teach as people and as learners will give us the information we need to be an effective decision maker in the classroom. With the information you learn from observing them, you can select the right materials, plan appropriate activities and ask questions that guide children in learning to understand the world around them' (Ellison, 2001).

It is easy to pass judgements on children because of isolated incidents, but this is like judging a picture from a few pieces of unconnected jigsaw. To get the whole picture we need to put together as many pieces as possible in the appropriate places.

Observation, carried out over time, reveals that first impressions can be wrong. It is important to observe children in different learning contexts, at different times of the day, while they are on task, when they are off task, during class and breaks, when they are with a group they are comfortable with and when they are with children with whom they are not familiar. It all depends upon the purpose of our observation. The point we make here is to be careful and to withhold from making any judgement until we are clear about our thoughts and perceptions.

An effective way of observation is what Jablon *et al.* (2007) call 'planned observation', where the teacher or the caregiver sets aside a period of free time every day to observe specific children. Observation here is part of the daily lesson plan and the teacher needs to be clear of her purpose of observation. The selection of the time and context of the observation is according to the purpose that the teacher has in mind.

Another kind of observation is more spontaneous, where for one reason or another, the teacher decides to stop whatever she is doing and observe. Some of these situations might be very precious opportunities that shouldn't be missed as they might provide us with invaluable insights about the child.

You can observe the children while they are on task or in action. This can tell us a lot about their attitude towards learning, their areas of strength and weaknesses and their work habits, and how they interact with other children. All this information is a real asset for you as a teacher in helping you to understand the children and can enable you to choose the time and strategies that are suitable for each child to further enhance their development in the different areas needed.

While observing children it is vital that you are as objective as possible. We all observe the world from our own perspective as we all have different schemata shaped by our background and experiences, yet our attempts at being objective and empathic can help to see the children through more filtered lenses. Understanding children is not always an easy task yet it can be a very rewarding one, especially when we use the results of the data we gather from observation to help the children flourish on different levels, emotionally, socially, academically and even physically.

The art of observation

Observing children is an art by itself. A good teacher is a good photographer who has her camera ready to take the right shots once she comes across them. She trains her eyes to look for moments of joy and achievement as well as moments of despair and struggle. She takes beautiful shots of children when they smile, when they play enthusiastically, when they take pride in their work, when they can work independently, or even when they giggle over a silly incident. She also takes shots when they do something of concern; when they feel isolated, when they struggle with a task, when they can't handle their relationships with others or when they look overwhelmed with their own issues. Once you practise this over a long period, it can then become a habit of mind. A skill that is indispensable and that can lead into having sharper pictures of the children we care for.

One of the beautiful outcomes of continuous child observation is that it helps the teacher to connect to the child, to feel the child, to be empathic, care genuinely and build a positive relationship with the child. Once this is achieved a more positive learning outcome can be expected as the child's brain will be more receptive to learning as 'learning is bonded with emotions' (Ellison 2001: 45).

How can we record our observation?

To ensure that you can get the best out of your observation, you need to record your observation in a systematic manner. You can record your observation in a way that feels most comfortable to you, yet all notes must be written in a non-judgemental way. You must train yourself to write notes as factual, descriptive information, with examples when possible. You also need to be flexible, as new information gathered in an observation can prove wrong information recorded earlier.

There are different tools that you can use to record information. Some teachers might feel comfortable with notepads, others might prefer to use Post-it notes, index cards, computer labels placed on a clipboard, anecdotal notes, matrices or even laptops or computers in the more fortunate situations. It all depends on what is available. It also depends on your style of note-taking.

Once enough information is gathered, then it is time for reflection and analysing the situations. The results here will lead you to plan for each child's development in whatever area is required.

Obviously, no real development can take place without parental involvement. Hence, once you put the pieces together and form a clear picture of the child, you can hold a conference with the parent or the caregiver to further discuss the child and plan together towards achieving the targets you agree upon.

Please note we are not recommending here that you leave parental involvement until the last stage in the process of observation. On the contrary, we believe that the earlier parents are involved the sooner the picture gets clear, yet this decision lies ultimately with your judgement.

Putting it into practice

Using an observation checklist

An observation checklist is a very useful tool that you can use to focus on or to gather data about specific children. The design can be a simple form that doesn't require much writing from the teacher (see below). Here are a few suggestions on how to use checklists:

1. Look at your class list and divide the children into groups for observation purposes.
2. Plan to observe each child once or twice a week, depending on your class size and your purpose of observation.

3. Design your checklist according to the purpose of your observation. You may have a set of common observation objectives for the whole class or you might need to have different objectives for different children.

4. After deciding on your objectives, break them down into specific behaviours or skill indicators.

5. Observe the child over a reasonable period until you develop a clear picture, then decide on the rating scale.

6. Add any comments you find important.

7. Repeat using the checklist over a period to find any pattern in child's behaviour.

8. Use the information you gather to plan how to help the child.

9. Use the checklist again to record child's progress.

10. Share the data you have with the parents.

11. If necessary, add a section where you can write your comments after meeting with the parents.

12. Keep all observation checklists in the child's portfolio to have a continuous record of the child's progress.

CHILD'S OBSERVATION CHECKLIST

Student's Name: _____ Class: _____ Date: _____

Aim of observation: to observe anger management skills

Rating Scale

3 Outstanding **2** Satisfactory **1** Needs improvement **X** Not Enough Opportunity to Observe

Emotional literacy	Rating Scale			Teacher's Comments
Skill Indicators The child:	1	2	3	
Knows what makes him angry				
Has good self-awareness when he feels angry				
Knows how to express his anger in a positive way				
Knows how to manage his anger				
Area of Improvement				
Teacher's Signature				

Figure 14: Child's observation checklist from *Life Skills 1 Assessment Guide* by Shahnaz Bahman.

Filming children

Using video to film children in their natural learning or play environment can be a great resource for you, especially when you find it difficult to observe, take notes, record progress and carry out all other tasks in class. You may then choose to use this recording or parts of it for further reflection or discussion with parents if the situation requires. Showing video clips to the children themselves in order to build up their reflective and problem-solving skills is another useful tool.

Being in disguise/wearing masks

Some children feel more comfortable expressing themselves when they don't face their teacher or any audience directly. Therefore, creating observation opportunities where children feel safe to express themselves under a cover or behind a mask can be very useful and rewarding. Role-play, costume parties and puppet shows can all help in this respect.

Recommended reading

Costa, A. L. and Kallick, B. (2000) *Habits of Mind*. Alexandria, VA: Association for Supervision and Curriculum Development.

Ellison, L. (1993) *Seeing With Magic Glasses*. Atlanta, GA: Great Ocean.

Jablon, Judy R., Dombro, Amy Laura, Dichtelmiller, Margo L. (2007) *The Power of Observation: Teaching Strategies*. National Association for the Education of Young Children.

Pianta, R. (2000) *Enhancing Relationships: Between Children and Teachers*. Washington, DC: American Psychological Association.

Rusnak, T. (1998) *An Integrated Approach to Character Education*. Thousand Oaks, CA: Corwin Press.

Reflective questions

1. What kind of questions would you ask yourself while observing a child?

2. Would you like to share a story that indicates some kind of change in your perception after observing a child?

3. What is the relationship between observation and teaching?

4. What can observation tell you about the children you teach?

5. What can observation tell you about what children are learning?

6. How can observation contribute to building a better relationship with the children you teach?

17 Where to Start

You see things; and you say 'Why?' But I dream things that never were; and I say 'Why not?'

George Bernard Shaw

A bird doesn't sing because it has an answer, it sings because it has a song.

Maya Angelou

The journey is the reward.

Chinese Proverb

Education ... a journey not a race.

Unknown

Now that you have read about the tools and strategies that we have used in the past chapters you may be wondering – where do I start? We suggest you start with small, easy steps with a big goal in mind!

Bringing emotional intelligence to your classroom is one of the most wonderful things you can do for the children in your classes. Those children who face so many struggles and problems in today's society deserve the opportunity to learn the skills that will help them prosper and do well in life. A favourite quote of ours is from Elizabeth Kubler Ross who said 'People are like stained-glass windows. They sparkle and shine when the sun is out, but when the darkness sets in, their true beauty is revealed only if there is a light from within.' As teachers we need to reach in for that light and light up the lives of the children in our care and try to help them overcome any darkness and negativity in their lives.

We recommend you study the SEL Implementation and Sustainability Process model shown below, Figure 15, from Devaney *et al.* (2006) which is a whole-school plan to integrate and value social emotional learning in the school. However, even if

Figure 15: Devaney, E., O'Brien, M.U., Resnik, H., Keister, S. and Weissberg, R. P. (2006) *Sustainable school-wide social and emotional learning (SEL): Implementation guide and toolkit.* Chicago: Collaborative for Academic, Social and Emotional Learning (CASEL). (Reprinted with permission)

your school is not yet ready to launch into a whole-school initiative, you as an individual teacher can still make a difference in your own classroom. Look at the model and think about steps that you can take today and tomorrow to make sure your classroom gives children the best chance of a happy, healthy life. Perhaps you can write an action plan for yourself with SMART goals; these can be small steps leading towards a bigger achievement.

When reading a book or hearing about a new concept it is easy to feel over-whelmed and then do nothing, but small steps are all that is needed to bring in major change. As a teacher, you may think 'How can I do all this and still cover the curriculum and ensure the children do well on standardized tests?'

We recommend the following ideas:

1. Make the decision to integrate EQ into your daily classroom practice.

2. Take steps to develop your own EQ skills by following the advice in Chapter 2.

3. Start a group with likeminded teachers who are interested in exploring EQ in the classroom. Set a

meeting time once or twice a month to discuss chapters of this and other books, and to produce further ideas.

4. When planning lessons, determine if there is a way to bring in aspects of emotional intelligence. For example, in language arts you can make emotional connections with the literature, you can explore others points of view. Literature gives us many lessons and opportunities to exploit EQ themes. In speaking and listening why not debate different points of view about issues in the news? In history, can you promote empathy by imagining what it was like to be a slave or a politician who had to make a tough decision? You can infuse EQ skills and expression of emotions into music, art and drama as we have shown in the earlier chapters in this book. Be creative and you will find many of the activities you do in your class can promote EQ.

5. Look at the everyday opportunities to bring EQ into your classroom. Besides the activities listed in this book, generally being aware of EQ issues and of the children's self-esteem, emotional well-being and feelings will help you to take opportunities to address these issues.

6. Often we are too busy concentrating on 'the curriculum' to take the opportunities available to enhance EQ skills. A news story about a natural disaster, an argument among the children, a new member of the class, a visit to a local hospital, a new sibling for one of your students or the death of a pet are all opportunities for you as a teacher to help build the skills and strategies needed in the real world. Take each of them and explore them.

Remember that you can make a difference. You can be one of the teachers whose children look back years from now and say 'Ms [*insert your name here*] was the teacher who inspired me or changed my life!' As Stephen Covey said, 'Believe in other people even if they don't believe in themselves. Listen to them and empathise with them. Help them to affirm their positive traits.' By giving children the gift of emotional intelligence, you help prepare them for a future when those skills will be critical for success. Go on, be the teacher they all remember! Make a difference! We end with a quote from Mahatma Ghandi: 'You may never know what results come of your action, but if you do nothing there will be no result!'

References

Antidote. (2003) *The Emotional Literacy Handbook*. London: David Fulton Publishers.

Bahman, S. (2007) *Life Skills 1 Assessment Guide*. Bahrain: Self-published.

Bourgeois, P. (1997) *Franklin's New Friend*. Toronto, ON: Kids Can Press.

Carlson, N. (1990) *I like Me*. Parsippany, NJ: Pearson Education.

Carlsson-Paige, N., and Lantieri, L. (2005) 'A changing vision of education', *Reclaiming Children and Youth*, 14.

Collaborative for Academic, Social and Emotional Learning (CASEL) (2007) 'What is SEL: Skills and Competencies'. Accessed 7 April 2007, from www.casel.org/basics/skills.php

Coetzee, M. and Jansen, C. (2007) *Emotional Intelligence in the Classroom*. Capetown: Juta.

Comer, J. P. (1984, May) 'Home–school relationships as they affect the academic success of children', *Education and Urban Society*, 16(3), 323–37.

Cooper, R. (1996) *Executive EQ: Emotional Intelligence in Leadership and Organizations*. New York: Berkeley.

Covey, S. (1992) *Principle-centered Leadership* (Fireside edition). New York: Simon & Schuster.

Dettore, E., and Cleary, S. (1997/98) 'Nurturing and strengthening emotional intelligence', *PAEYC Newsletter*, December/January, 7–8.

Devaney, E., O'Brien, M.U., Resnik, H., Keister, S. and Weissberg, R.P. (2006). *Sustainable schoolwide social and emotional learning (SEL): Implementation guide and toolkit*. Chicago: Collaborative for Academic, Social and Emotional Learning (CASEL).

Doty, G. (2001) *Fostering Emotional Intelligence in K-8 students*. Thousand Oaks, CA: Corwin Press.

Elias, M. J., Arnold, H. and Hussey, C. S. (2003) *EQ+IQ; Best Leadership Practices for Caring and Successful Schools*. Thousand Oaks, CA: Corwin Press.

Ellison, L. (2001) *The Personal Intelligences*. Thousand Oaks, CA: Corwin Press.

Francis, M. E. and Pennebaker, J. W. (1991) 'Putting stress into words: the impact of writing on physiological, absentee and self-reported emotional wellbeing measures', *American Journal of Health Promotion*, 6, 280–7.

Freedman, J. and Jensen, A. (2005) *EQ Trainer Certification Manual*. San Mateo, CA: Six Seconds.

Gardner, H. (1983) *Frames of Mind; The Theory of Multiple Intelligences*. New York: Basic Books.

Goleman, D. (1995) *Emotional Intelligence: Why it can Matter More than IQ*. New York: Bantam.

Gottman, J. (1997) *Raising an Emotionally Intelligent Child*. New York: Fireside.

Greenspan, S. (1997) *The Growth of the Mind*. Reading, MA: Addison-Wesley.

Hanser, S. B. (1985) 'Music therapy and stress reduction research', *Journal of Music Therapy*, 22, 193–201.

Henniger, M. L. (1999) *Teaching young children: An introduction*. Upper Saddle River, NJ: Prentice-Hall.

Herbert, T. P. and Furner, J. M. (1997) 'Helping high ability students overcome math anxiety through bibliotherapy', *Journal of Secondary Gifted Education*, 8 164–79.

Hoover-Dempsey, K.V. and Sandler, H. M. (1997) 'Why do parents become involved in their children's education?', *Review of Educational Research*, 67, 3–42.

Ingram, M. A. (2003) 'The use of sociocultural poetry to assist gifted students in developing empathy for the lived experiences of others', *Journal of Secondary Gifted Education*, 14.

Jablon, J. R., Dombro, A. L. and Dichtelmiller, M. L. (2007) *The Power of Observation*. Washington, DC: Teaching Strategies.

Jensen, E. (2005) *Teaching with the Brain in Mind*. Alexandria, VA: Association for Supervision and Curriculum Development.

Jewett, J. (1997) 'Childhood stress', *Childhood Education*, 73, 172–3.

Johnson, C. E., Wan, G., Templeton, R. A., Graham, L. P. and Sattler, J. L. (2000) '"Booking it" to peace: bibliotherapy guidelines for teachers', *ERIC Clearinghouse on Bibliotherapy*.

Kaufman, G., Raphael, L. and Esplenad, P. (1999). *Stick up for Yourself*, Minneapolis, MN: Free Spirit Publishing.

Kerr, T., Walsh, J. and Marshall, A. (2001). 'Emotional change processes in music-assisted reframing', *The Journal of Music Therapy*, 38(3), 193–211.

Ladd, G. W., Kochenderfer, B. J. and Coleman, C. C. (1997). 'Classroom peer acceptance, friendship and victimization: distinct relational systems that contribute uniquely to children's school adjustment?', *Child Development*, 68(6), 1,181–97.

LeDoux, J. (1996) *The Emotional Brain: The Mysterious Underpinnings of Emotional Life*. New York: Touchstone. ED, 451–622.

Littky, D. with Grabelle, S. (2004). *The Big Picture*. Alexandria, VA: Association for Supervision and Curriculum Development.

McCown, K. S., Freedman, J. M., Jensen, A. L. and Rideout, M. C. (1998) *Self Science; The Emotional Intelligence Curriculum*. San Mateo, CA: Six Seconds.

Magrath, J. (2007, June) 'Polyphony', *American Music Teacher*, 56(6), 80.

Masurel, C. (2001) *Two Homes*. Cambridge, MA: Candlewick.

Mayer, J., and Salovey, P. (1997) 'What is emotional intelligence?', in J. D. Mayer and P. Salvoey (eds), *Emotional Development and Emotional Intelligence*, New York: Basic Books.

Morris, E. and Casey, J. (2006) *Developing Emotional Literate Staff – a Practical Guide*. London: Paul Chapman.

Moses, B. (1997), *I'm Lonely (Your Feelings)*. London: Hodder Wayland.

Nabuzoka, D. and Smith, K. (1995) 'Identification of expressions of emotions by children with and without learning disabilities', *Learning Disabilities Research and Practice*, 10, 91–101.

NAPT (1997) *The National Association for Poetry Therapy Guide to Training*. New York: NAPT.

National Research Council and Institute of Medicine (2000) *From Neurons to Neighbourhoods: The Science of Early Childhood Development*. Washington, DC: National Academy Press.

Olness, R. (2007) *Using Literature to Enhance Content Area: Instruction Guide for K-5 Teachers*. USA: International Reading Association.

Ouzts, D. T. (1991) 'The emergence of bibliotherapy as a discipline', *Reading Horizons*, 31, 199–206.

Palmer, P. (1998) *The Courage to Teach*. San Francisco, CA: Jossey-Bass.

Pardeck J. T. (1989) 'Bibliotherapy: a tool for helping preschool children deal with developmental change related to family relationships', *Early Child Development and Care*, 47, 107–29. EJ 401 179.

Pardeck, J. T. (1994) 'Using literature to help adolescents cope with problems', *Adolescence*, 29(114), 421–7.

Pennebaker, J. W. (1997) 'Writing about emotional experiences as a therapeutic process', *Psychological Science*, 8, 162–5.

Pennebaker, J. W. and Francis, M. E. (1996) 'Cognitive, emotional and language processes in disclosure', *Cognition and Emotion*, 10, 601–26.

Pennebaker, J. W. and Seagal, J. D. (1999) 'Forming a story: the health benefits of narrative', *Journal of Clinical Psychology*, 55, 1, 243–54.

Petrides, K., Frederickson, N. and Furnham, A. (2004) 'The role of trait emotional intelligence in academic performance and deviant behaviour at school', *Personality and Individual Differences*, 36, 277–93.

Pouliot, J. (1998) 'The power of music', *World and I*, 13(5), 146.

Rich, D. (1988) 'Bridging the parent gap in education reform', *Educational Horizons*, 66(2), 90–2.

Riley, S. (1999) *Contemporary Art Therapy with Adolescents*. London: Jessica Kingsley.

Scieszka, J. (1995) *The True Story of the Three Little Pigs*. New York: Puffin Books.

Sharma, R. (1997) *The Monk who sold his Ferrari*. New York: HarperCollins.

Sharp, P. (2001) *Nurturing Emotional Literacy – A practical guide for teachers, parents and those in the caring profession*. London: David Fulton.

Shonkoff, J. (2007) 'The good, the bad, and the tolerable: how different stress levels impact the brain.' Accessed 1 June 2007 from www.uknow.gse.harvard.edu/learning/LD102-507.htm

Simich-Dudgeon, C. (1986) 'Parent involvement and the education of limited-English-proficient students', *ERIC Digest*. Washington, DC: Center for Applied Linguistics.

Spelman, C. M. (2001) *Mama and Daddy Bear's Divorce*. Morton Grove, IL: Albot Whitman & Company.

Stroud, J. E., Stroud, J. C. and Staley, L. M. (1999) 'Adopted children in the early childhood classroom', *ERIC Clearinghouse on Elementary and Early Childhood Education*. (ERIC Document Reproduction Service no. ED 426–819).

Sylwester, R. (1997a) *A celebration of neurons: An educator's guide to the human brain*. Alexandria, VA: Association for Supervision and Curriculum Development.

Sylwester, R. (1997b) 'Electronic media and brain development' (Video). Tuscon, AZ: Zephyr.

Sylwester, R. (1998, November) 'Art of the brain's sake', *Educational Leadership*, 31–5.

Weare, K. (2004) *Developing the Emotionally Literate School*. London: Sage.

Appendix: Emotional Literacy Bank

It is often difficult for us to address specific feelings and emotions because we find it difficult to put them into words. Building up our knowledge and understanding of vocabulary related to emotions is a crucial step to improving our emotional literacy. The list of words below may help you as a teacher to use the words yourself and expand the vocabulary of the children in your class as well. Depending on the age of the children, you may wish to introduce and explain some or all of the words below. It is very useful for children to create an emotional literacy dictionary or log where they can write down new words they hear that relate to feelings and emotions. They can then refer back to these words when writing in journals or in other activities.

angry	antagonistic	confused	cruel
aggravated	apprehensive	confident	cheery
aggressive	anxious	careful	cross
argumentative	bored	contented	charitable
ashamed	bothered	cautious	depressed
alert	bewildered	concerned	delighted
assured	belligerent	conviction	discontented
assertive	baffled	confused	dissatisfied
attentive	brave	courteous	dumbfounded
afraid	bold	considerate	distress
aware	breathtaking	civil	distrustful
alarmed	brilliant	confrontational	doubtful
amazed	brutal	conscientious	disbelieving
annoyed	bemused	courageous	despondent
astonishing	befuddled	calm	destructive
amused	belief	cool	dejected
astound	caring	composed	devoted

disturbed	furious	jaded	privileged
dazed	grim	jolly	positive
down	gracious	jubilant	pleasant
dubious	gleeful	jittery	powerful
drained	glad	jovial	pushy
dull	great	kind	perceptive
disgust	guarded	lively	protected
drained	grand	love	preoccupied
embarrassed	good-natured	livid	panicked
encouraging	gutsy	low	puzzled
energetic	grumpy	leery	quiet
easy-going	grouchy	lonely	queer
exasperated	gentle	lethargic	quarrelsome
excite	grieve	mad	reluctant
elated	happy	magnificent	riled
edgy	hopeful	miserable	relaxed
empathy	humbling	mystified	restless
enraged	heartening	mortified	refreshed
enlightened	harsh	melancholic	resourceful
envy	horrified	mad	receptive
exposed	hopeless	mournful	responsive
fulfilled	helpful	merry	responsible
furious	hesitant	naughty	sorry
flabbergast	humiliated	neglectful	sad
frightened	hurt	neurotic	susceptible
faith	hostile	nervous	stroppy
fed up	indifferent	negative	shattered
fascinated	ideological	numb	spirited
frustrated	inconsiderate	nasty	sadistic
fretful	impatient	offend	sceptical
fatigued	infuriated	outraged	scared
fantastic	inhuman	optimistic	sleepy
fearful	insightful	overwhelmed	sorrow
forlorn	indifferent	pessimistic	surprised
friendly	irritated	peaceful	stunned
frazzled	intense	perturbed	shaken
fierce	irate	petrified	surprise
fretful	incensed	passive	stressed
forceful	jealous	proud	strained
fuming	joy	praised	startled

shock	satisfied	trust	unhappy
splendid	successful	tired	uninterested
sure	triumphant	tense	vicious
stun	tense	tolerant	vulnerable
stagger	timid	uptight	violent
safe	traumatized	uncomfortable	vexed
shocked	thoughtful	uneasy	weary
selfless	thriving	unruffled	worried
sensitive	tranquil	understanding	wonderful
secure	terrified	upset	
sheltered	troubled	unruly	
suspicious	tremendous	uplifting	

Index

(whole chapter or section references in **bold**)

emotional development *see also* emotional
    intelligence *and* EQ
  in early childhood **3–4**
  in elementary school **4–5**
Emotional Intelligence (Goleman) 3, 89
emotional intelligence 2–4, 7, 14,16, 22, 30,
    37, 45, 57, 61, 63–4, 68, 70, 75–6, 78,
    82, 88, 96, 98–100, 114, 116 *see also*
    emotional development *and* EQ
  in teachers **6–17**
  and empathy **13–15**
  and managing emotions **9–11**
  and relationships **15–17**
  and self-awareness **7–9**
  and self-motivation **11–13**
  practices
  first application of **114–16**
empathy 3, 5, 14, 16, 26, 46, 52–3, 57, 60–1,
    63–6, 72, 75–6, 79, 93, 98, 116
EQ 2–3, 5, 14, 27, 32, 40, 43, 46, 54–5,
    59–60, 63, 66, 69, 71–2, 74–5, 78, 80,
    85, 89–90, 92–3, 95–6, 98–9, 102,
    106, 115–16 *see also* emotional
    development *and* emotional
    intelligence
  definition of 3
  development of 3
Ellison, L. 7–8, 12, 16, 30–1, 43, 102,
    108–9

families 94, 95, 98
fatigue 10
fear 4, 9, 20, 52, 54, 82, 103 *see also* afraid
    and scared
feeling thermometer **31–2**, 33
'flow' 11, 13
Frames of Mind 3
Freedman, J. and Jensen, A. 3
friendship 4–5, 25, 92

Gardner, Howard 3
Ghandi, Mahatma 11, 17, 116
Goleman, Daniel 3–4, 7–9, 11, 13–16, 30–1,
    36, 43, 49, 58, 60, 75–6, 89
Gottman, John 37–8
Greenspan, S. 30

Habits of Mind 102
happiness 4–5, 31, 33, 38–9, 69, 81, 85 *see*
    also happy

happy *see also* happiness
  children 10, 19, 27, 30–1, 33, 38–9, 45, 57,
    71, 115
  teachers 7, 15, 24
home–school links **94–100**
  and family circle time 98
  and family treasure box 96
  and making parents welcome **95–6**
  and newsletters 98
Hoover-Dempsey, K. V. and Sandler, H. M. 95

I'm Lonely (Your Feelings) 59
insecure 14, 19, 21, 30
Ireland, G. O. 57

Jablon, Judy R. et al. 108
jealousy 52, 69, 71
Jensen, E. 4, 36
journal(ing) 6, 9, 12, 26, 36, **48–55**, 59–60,
    63, 90, 103–5, 108
  and current events 52
  and emotional quotes 52
  and emotional intelligence quotes **52–3**
  and journal prompts **53–4**
  and self-learning **49–50**
  and small groups 53

Kaufman, G., Raphael, L. and Esplenad, P. 36
Kubler Ross, Elizabeth 114

learning 1–2, 7, 11, 1314, 16, 19–20, 22,
    24–5, 27, 30, 36–8, 42–3, 49, 89–90, 93,
    103, 105, 107–9, 112–13
  community 12
  contexts 108
  environment (positive) **18–28**
  and child–teacher relationship **20**
  and choice for children 24
  and classroom rules 22
  and class routines 24
  and peer relationships 21
  experience 21, 89–90, 102
  opportunities 11, 12–13, 22, 89
  outcomes 14, 21–2, 24, 32, 109
  process 14, 16, 21, 24, 30, 32, 89
  social and emotional 2, 27, 46, 102,
    114–15
  styles 24

Mama and Daddy Bear's Divorce 59

songs and music **69–73** *see also* song *and* music
  and emotional intelligence songs **71–2**
  and listening **71**
songs and music—*cont.*
  and making music **72**
  and making songs **72**
  and musical feelings **71**
  and self-expression **70**
Spelman, Cornelia Maude 59
Stick up for Yourself 36
storytelling **56–61**, 102 *see also* bibliotherapy
stress 9–10, 13, 21, 24, 32, 35, 49–50, 70, 75, 81–2, 98
  and effect on learning **36–7**

-free 41
levels 41
stress relief **36–41**, 54
  activities **37–40**
  and deep breathing **39**
  and meditation **38–9**
  and the throw away **40**
Sylwester, Robert 43, 104

trust 13, 20, 44, 46, 69, 89, 103
Two Homes 59

unhappy 34, 101 *see also* sad *and* sadness

values 11–12, 15, 19, 33, 58, 68
Van Gogh 18, 85

DATE DUE